ELEMENTARY
Grammar Practice Book

in
English

PETER VINEY
KAREN VINEY

OXFORD
UNIVERSITY PRESS

OXFORD
UNIVERSITY PRESS

Great Clarendon Street, Oxford OX2 6DP

Oxford University Press is a department of the University of Oxford.
It furthers the University's objective of excellence in research, scholarship,
and education by publishing worldwide in

Oxford New York

Auckland Cape Town Dar es Salaam Hong Kong Karachi
Kuala Lumpur Madrid Melbourne Mexico City Nairobi
New Delhi Shanghai Taipei Toronto

With offices in

Argentina Austria Brazil Chile Czech Republic France Greece
Guatemala Hungary Italy Japan Poland Portugal Singapore
South Korea Switzerland Thailand Turkey Ukraine Vietnam

OXFORD and OXFORD ENGLISH are registered trade marks of
Oxford University Press in the UK and in certain other countries

© Oxford University Press / Three Vee Limited 2004

The moral rights of the author have been asserted

Database right Oxford University Press (maker)

First published 2004
2014 2013 2012 2011
10 9 8 7

No unauthorized photocopying

All rights reserved. No part of this publication may be reproduced,
stored in a retrieval system, or transmitted, in any form or by any means,
without the prior permission in writing of Oxford University Press,
or as expressly permitted by law, or under terms agreed with the appropriate
reprographics rights organization. Enquiries concerning reproduction
outside the scope of the above should be sent to the ELT Rights Department,
Oxford University Press, at the address above

You must not circulate this book in any other binding or cover
and you must impose this same condition on any acquirer

Any websites referred to in this publication are in the public domain and
their addresses are provided by Oxford University Press for information only.
Oxford University Press disclaims any responsibility for the content

ISBN-13: 978 0 19 437537 5

Typeset in Meta

Printed in China

ACKNOWLEDGEMENTS
Designed by Richard Morris, Stonesfield Design

Contents

Grammar tables 4
How to use this book 8
Practice 9
Answer key 70
Audio exercises 79

Language words

Grammar word	Examples
article	a, an, the
noun	woman, apple, car, pen, town, knife
verb (main verb)	listen, look, walk, go, write
auxiliary verb	am, is, are, do, does, did, have, has
modal	can, must, could, will, won't, would
adjective	large, blue, cold, English, French
comparative	larger, bigger, more important, better, worse
superlative	largest, biggest, most important, best, worst
subject pronoun	I, you, he, she, it, we, they
object pronoun	me, you, him, her, it, us, them
possessive adjective	my, your, his, her, its, our, their
indefinite pronoun	something, anything, nothing, somewhere, anybody, no one
demonstrative	this, that, these, those
frequency adverb	always, usually, often, sometimes, hardly ever, never
adverb of manner	quickly, slowly, well, badly, fast
possessive (nouns)	David's, Maria's, Charles's, the boys'
preposition	in, on, off, by, near
singular (1)	pen, watch, apple, man, child
plural (2 +)	pens, watches, apples, men, children
contraction	I'm, we're, I'd, he's, they've, can't, hasn't, haven't, don't, doesn't, didn't, couldn't, wouldn't, I'll, I won't
vowel	a, e, i, o, u, (y)
consonant	b, c, d, f, g, h, j, k, l, m, n, p, q, r, s, t, v, w, x, y, z
small letters	a, b, c ...
capital letters	A, B, C ...
numbers	1, 2, 3, 4 ...
ordinal numbers	1st, 2nd, 3rd, 4th ...
punctuation	, . ? ! / " : ; ( )
conversation	A: How are you?
	B: I'm fine. And you?
tense	past, present, future
aspect	present simple, present continuous, present perfect
determiner	article, demonstrative, possessive adjective

Sounds

Vowels

iː	s**ee**	/siː/	ʌ	c**u**p	/kʌp/
i	happ**y**	/'hæpi/	ɜː	th**ir**d	/θɜːd/
ɪ	s**i**t	/sɪt/	ə	**a**bout	/ə'baʊt/
e	t**e**n	/ten/	eɪ	d**ay**	/deɪ/
æ	h**a**t	/hæt/	əʊ	g**o**	/gəʊ/
ɑː	f**a**ther	/'fɑːðə(r)/	aɪ	f**i**ve	/faɪv/
ɒ	g**o**t	/gɒt/	aʊ	n**ow**	/naʊ/
ɔː	f**ou**r	/fɔː(r)/	ɔɪ	b**oy**	/bɔɪ/
ʊ	f**oo**t	/fʊt/	ɪə	n**ea**r	/nɪə(r)/
u	sit**u**ation	/sɪtʃu'eɪʃn/	eə	p**ai**r	/peə(r)/
uː	t**oo**	/tuː/	ʊə	t**ou**rist	/'tʊərɪst/

Consonants

p	**p**en	/pen/	s	**s**o	/səʊ/
b	**b**ad	/bæd/	z	**z**oo	/zuː/
t	**t**ea	/tiː/	ʃ	**sh**oe	/ʃuː/
d	**d**id	/dɪd/	ʒ	televi**si**on	/telɪ'vɪʒn/
k	**c**at	/kæt/	h	**h**ad	/hæd/
g	**g**ot	/gɒt/	m	**m**an	/mæn/
tʃ	**ch**air	/tʃeə(r)/	n	**n**o	/nəʊ/
dʒ	**J**une	/dʒuːn/	ŋ	si**ng**	/sɪŋ/
f	**f**ive	/faɪv/	l	**l**eft	/left/
v	**v**an	/væn/	r	**r**ed	/red/
θ	**th**ank	/θæŋk/	j	**y**es	/jes/
ð	**th**is	/ðɪs/	w	**w**e	/wiː/

Irregular verbs

present	past	past participle	present	past	past participle
am, is, are	was, were	been	has, have	had	had
buy	bought	bought	know	knew	known
come	came	come	make	made	made
do, does	did	done	put	put	put
get	got	got	see	saw	seen
go	went	gone	take	took	taken

Verbs

verb form	positive	negative
present: *be*	I'm He's / She's / It's We're / You're / They're	I'm not He / She / It isn't We / You / They aren't
present continuous: *do*	I'm doing He's / She's / It's doing We're / You're / They're doing	I'm not doing He / She / It isn't doing We / You / They aren't doing
future: *going to*	I'm going to (do) He / She / It's going to (do) We / You / They're going to (do)	I'm not going to (do) He / She / It isn't going to (do) We / You / They aren't going to (do)
past simple: *be*	I / He / She / It was We / You / They were	I / He / She / It wasn't We / You / They weren't
have got	I / We / You / They've got He / She / It's got	I / We / You / They haven't got He / She / It hasn't got
imperative	Do (this). Be (quiet).	Don't do (that). Don't be (silly).
present simple: *do*	I / We / You / They do He / She / It does	I / We / You / They don't do He / She / It doesn't do
past simple: *do*	I / He / She / It / We / You / They did	I / He / She / It / We / You / They didn't do
present perfect: *do*	I / We / You / They have done He / She / It has done	I / We / You / They haven't done He / She / It hasn't done
can	I / He / She / It / We / You / They can (do)	I / He / She / It / We / You / They can't (do)
would like	I / He / She / It / We / You / They 'd like	I / He / She / It / We / You / They wouldn't like
will	I / He / She / It / We / You / They will (do)	I / He / She / It / We / You / They won't like (do)

question	short answer
Am I ...? Is he/she/it ...? Are we/you/they ...?	Yes, I am. / No, I'm not. Yes, she is. / No, she isn't. Yes, we are. / No, we aren't.
Am I doing ...? Is he/she/it doing ...? Are we/you/they doing ...?	Yes, I am. / No, I'm not. Yes, she is. / No, she isn't. Yes, we are. / No, we aren't.
Am I going to (do) ...? Is he/she/it going to (do) ...? Are we/you/they going to (do) ...?	Yes, I am. / No, I'm not. Yes, she is. / No, she isn't. Yes, we are. / No, we aren't.
Was I/he/she/it ...? Were we/you/they ...?	Yes, I was. / No, I wasn't. Yes, we were. / No, we weren't.
Have I/we/you/they got ...? Has he/she/it got ...?	Yes, I have. / No, I haven't. Yes, he has. / No, he hasn't.
– –	– –
Do we/you/they/I do ...? Does he/she/it do ...?	Yes, I do. / No, I don't. Yes, he does. / No, he doesn't.
Did I/he/she/it/we/you/they do ...?	Yes, I did. / No, I didn't.
Have I/we/you/they done ...? Has he/she/it done ...?	Yes, I have. / No, I haven't. Yes, she has. / No, she hasn't.
Can I/he/she/it/we/you/they (do) ...?	Yes, I can. / No, I can't.
Would I/he/she/it/we/you/they like ...?	Yes, I would. / No, I wouldn't.
Will I/he/she/it/we/you/they (do) ...?	Yes, I will. / No, I won't.

How to use this book

- One Practice unit for each Student's Book unit
- Audio exercises for each Student's Book unit
- Grammar tables for reference

After the class

Work on the Practice exercises:

You can think about the answer.

What's .... name?

You can write in the answer.

What's ..*her*.. name?

You can write the sentence again.

What's .... name?

What's her name?

Work on the Audio exercises:

You can listen to the audio exercises.

You can look at the book, listen, and repeat the audio exercises.

You can listen and repeat the audio exercises.

Practice

in English

one

Grammar: *be* singular

Complete the table.

Positive		Negative		Questions
full form	contraction	full form	contraction	
I am	I'm	I am not	I'm not	Am I ...?
You are	.....	You are not	You aren't	.....
He is	.....	He is not	.....	Is he ...?
She is	She's	She is not	.....	.....

Personal information

Put the words in the box on the hotel registration card.

Telephone number   First name   Nationality   Title   Family name

GRAND TOWERS HOTEL

....	*Mrs*
....	*Vargas*
....	*Maria*
....	*Spanish*
....	*(34) 93 456 7890*

Responses

Match.

1. Nice to meet you.
2. What's her name?
3. Where's she from?
4. Can you spell that?
5. What's his phone number?
6. See you later.

A Yes, see you.
B Sydney.
C 028 617 0954.
D Nice to meet you, too.
E Kylie.
F Yes. K-Y-L-I-E.

Numbers

Find the numbers 0–9.

- wot   *two*

A ERTHE   B GTIEH   C INNE   D NEESV   E VEIF
F RUFO   G IXS   H NEO   I OREZ

Writing: capital letters

Write the sentences with capital letters.
1 patrick's from dublin in ireland.
2 nice to meet you, josh.
3 london's in england.
4 pepsi is american.

Reading: countries and nationalities

Look at the picture. Circle the correct words.
1 *Seven Samurai* is a (Japan / Japanese) film by Kurosawa.
   The (America / American) film, *The Magnificent Seven* is the same story.
2 Bruce Springsteen is an (American / USA) songwriter.
   Born in (USA / the USA) is an album by Springsteen.
3 Franz Josef Liszt is the famous (Austria / Austrian) composer
   of (Hungary / Hungarian) Rhapsodies.
4 *From (Russia / Russian) With Love* is a book about the (English / England)
   spy, James Bond.
5 The stars of the film *The (Italy / Italian) Job* are the three cars.
   They're (Britain / British) Minis.
6 Asterix is a (France / French) cartoon character. In *Asterix and Cleopatra*
   he's in (Egypt / Egyptian) with the (Egypt / Egyptian) queen, Cleopatra.

two

Grammar: *be* plural

Complete the tables.

Positive		Negative		Questions
full form	contraction	full form	contraction	
We are	.....	We are not	.....	.....
You are	You're	You are not	You aren't	Are you ...?
They are	.....	They are not	.....	.....

subject pronoun	I	you	he	she	we	they
possessive adjective	my	.....	.....	.....	.....	.....

Short answers: *be*

Complete the short answers.
- Are you British? No, *I'm not*.
- Are they late? Yes, *they are*.

1 Is she married? No, ...
2 Are we students? Yes, ...
3 Are you a teacher? No, ...
4 Are you OK? Yes, ...
5 Is he single? Yes, ...
6 Are they American? No, ...
7 Is she from China? Yes, ...
8 Are they married? Yes, ...

Possessive adjectives

Complete the sentences.

- I'm David. *My name's David.*

1 You're Mrs Ashton. .... name's Mrs Ashton.
2 He's Kevin. .... name's Kevin.
3 They're Jenny and Kevin. .... names are Jenny and Kevin.
4 We're Peter and Karen. .... names are Peter and Karen.
5 She's Wendy. .... name's Wendy.

Numbers: date of birth

Write the numbers in words.

- 12/11/85   twelve / eleven / eighty-five

1 3/12/77 .... 4 16/1/03 .... 7 11/3/94 ....
2 21/8/01 .... 5 15/5/55 .... 8 13/4/68 ....
3 30/7/87 .... 6 22/2/99 .... 9 14/10/49 ....

Greetings

1 **Read.**
This is a postcard from Australia. 'G'day' (Good day) is an Australian greeting. It means *good morning*, or *good afternoon*, or *good evening*. 'Mate' means *friend*. You can find 'Good day' in old British and American books, but people don't say it now in Britain or North America.

2 **Put the words in the correct columns.**

Good morning. See you tonight. Hi! Bye. Good afternoon.
Good evening. Goodnight. See you. Hey!

'Hello' only	'Goodbye' only	'Hello' or 'Goodbye'

Responses

Match.

1 How old are you?   A Good evening, Mr Green.
2 How are you?   B Mind your own business!
3 Are you married?   C Fine, thanks.
4 What nationality are you?   D Twenty-one.
5 Where are you from?   E Chinese.
6 Are you rich?   F No, I'm single.
7 This is my father.   G China.

three

Grammar: a / an

1 Put *a* or *an* in the spaces.

1 ..... espresso
2 ..... pizza
3 ..... sandwich
4 ..... muffin
5 ..... American muffin
6 ..... egg sandwich
7 ..... iced coffee
8 ..... tuna sandwich
9 ..... large espresso
10 ..... almond Danish
11 ..... apple juice
12 ..... cup of tea

2 Are these statements true or false? Write T or F.

1 *a, e, i, o, u* are vowels.
2 *b, c, d, f, g, h, j, k, l, m, n, p, q, r, s, t, v, w, x, y, z* are consonants.
3 In words like *my, by, very* the letter *y* has a vowel sound.
4 Use *an* before the sound of a vowel.
5 Use *a* before the sound of a consonant.

Writing: question marks and full stops

? is a question mark.

. is a full stop (UK) or a period (USA).

Put question marks or full stops in the boxes.
1 'Anything else ☐' 'No, thanks ☐'
2 'Regular or large ☐' 'Regular, please ☐'
3 'How much is that ☐' 'Five thirty ☐'
4 'What's her name ☐' 'Anna ☐ Is she in your class ☐'
5 'That's sixteen twenty-five ☐' 'Sorry ☐ How much ☐'

and, or

Complete the sentences with *and* or *or*.

1. 'Single ..... double?' 'Double, please.'
2. An egg ..... tomato sandwich, please.
3. 'Apple juice ..... orange juice?' 'Apple, please.'
4. 'Milk ..... sugar?' 'Milk, please. No sugar.'
5. Two chocolate ..... one strawberry, please.
6. 'Black ..... white coffee?' 'White, please.'

Word + word

Read the restaurant signs.
1. Complete.
   Morning ....   Afternoon ....   Evening ....
2. Find words that go with: (a) lunch   (b) lunches.
3. Find words connected by '&'.
4. List the words for meals.
5. Find the international words (words that are the same, or nearly the same, in your language).

four

Grammar: demonstrative pronouns

1 Complete the table with *this, that, these, those*.

	near	far
singular		
plural		

2 Complete the table.

singular	lunch	painting	guide	seat	entrance	glass	potato
plural							

Responses

Match the questions and answers.

1 Who's it by?
2 Where are they?
3 How old are they?
4 What is it?
5 What colour is it?
6 How much are they?
7 How about a drink?

A Four hundred years old.
B Five sixty.
C Yes, please.
D An umbrella.
E Picasso.
F Light blue.
G In the bar.

Colours

Complete the sentences with colours.

1 '………… coffee or white coffee?'

2 Blue is for boys. ………… is for girls.

3 White + black = ………… .

4 ………… is for 'stop'. Green is for 'go'.

5 Red + yellow = ………… .

6 Red + blue = ………… .

7 *Casablanca* is an old black and ………… film.

8 '………… sugar or white sugar?'

9 The McDonald's logo is a ………… M.

10 The Italian flag is red, white, and ………… .

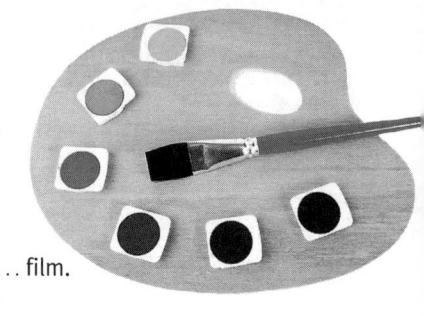

Numbers

Some numbers have *and* in them. Some numbers don't have *and* in them.

Put *and* in the correct places.
- Five hundred eighty-three   *Five hundred **and** eighty-three*
- Five thousand eight hundred   *Five thousand eight hundred*

1. Two hundred seventy-six
2. Forty-three thousand
3. Fifty seven
4. Three thousand four hundred five
5. Sixty-two thousand nine hundred sixty-one
6. One thousand five hundred

Quiz

1. **Complete the quiz with question words from the box.**

   Where   How old   Who   What colour   What

2. **Answer the quiz.**

1. .... are New York taxis?
   ☐ Black. ☐ Pink. ☐ Yellow.

2. .... is the play *Hamlet* by?
   ☐ William Shakespeare. ☐ Charles Dickens.
   ☐ Andrew Lloyd-Webber.

3. .... is British Columbia?
   ☐ In South America. ☐ In Canada.
   ☐ In the United Kingdom.

4. .... are the pyramids in Egypt?
   ☐ Four thousand years.
   ☐ Twenty thousand years.
   ☐ Five hundred years.

5. .... are The Rolling Stones from?
   ☐ The USA. ☐ England. ☐ Ireland.

6. .... is the capital city of Australia?
   ☐ Sydney. ☐ Melbourne. ☐ Canberra.

7. .... is Formula One?
   ☐ Motor-car racing. ☐ Bicycle racing. ☐ Horse racing.

8. .... nationality is the film star Leonardo diCaprio?
   ☐ Italian. ☐ English. ☐ American.

3. **Write a quiz with eight questions.**

five

Grammar: *have got / has got*

1 Complete the table.

Positive		Negative		Questions
full form	contraction	full form	contraction	
I have got	I've got	I have not got	I haven't got	Have I got ...?
You	.....	.....	.....	.....
We	.....	.....	.....	.....
They	.....	.....	.....	.....
He has got	.....	.....	.....	.....
She	.....	.....	.....	.....
It	.....	.....	.....	.....

2 Possessions. Look at the examples and make sentences.

1 a cat   2 sunglasses   3 a dictionary

David ✗ Anna ✓ You?   David ✓ Anna ✗ You?   David ✗ Anna ✗ You?

4 boots   5 gloves   6 a personal stereo

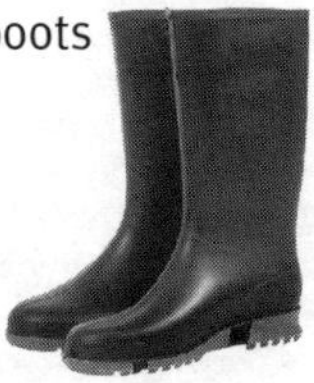

David ✗ Anna ✗ You?   David ✓ Anna ✓ You?   David ✗ Anna ✓ You?

1 *David hasn't got a cat. Anna's got a cat.*

   I ....

2 *David's got some sunglasses. Anna hasn't got any sunglasses.*

   I ....

3 ....

4 ....

5 ....

6 ....

Family words

Complete the table.

male	female
grandfather	grandmother
....	mother
....	aunt
husband	....
....	daughter
....	sister
....	niece
grandson	....

Responses

Match the questions and answers.

1 Have you got a light?
2 Have you got the time?
3 Can you describe her?
4 What's wrong?
5 Has she got a boyfriend?
6 Have you got any brothers or sisters?
7 Has Dr Smith got an appointment for today?

A She's got red hair and grey eyes.
B No, I'm an only child.
C I don't know. Ask her.
D Sorry. I don't smoke.
E Yes, it's twenty-five to three.
F Yes, she's free at three thirty.
G I've got a headache.

Writing: apostrophes

We use apostrophes (') in contractions for missing letters.
I've got a pen. = *I have got a pen.*   The missing letters are **ha**.
He's Spanish. = *He is Spanish.*   The missing letter is ***i***.

What are the missing letters in these sentences?

1 They've got two children.   ....
2 She's got some trainers.   ....
3 I don't know.   ....
4 They're from Los Angeles.   ....
5 I haven't got any brothers.   ....
6 We aren't English.   ....
7 That's my seat.   ....
8 I'm very well, thank you.   ....
9 What's your name?   ....

six

Grammar: present simple

Subject pronoun	Positive	Negative	Questions	Short answers
I, You, We, They	work	don't work	Do (you) work?	.....
	.....	don't sell	Do (you) sell?	No, (I) don't.
	know	.....	.....	
He, She, It	.....	.....	.....	Yes, (he) does.
	sells	doesn't sell	Does (he) sell?	No, (he) doesn't.
	knows	doesn't know	Does (he) know?	

1 Read the conversation and complete the table with the underlined words.

A Excuse me, is Claire Kelly here?
B Sorry, Claire <u>doesn't work</u> here now.
A Oh? Where <u>does she work</u>?
B She <u>works</u> in our Manchester office. Can I help you?
A Yes, I'm from ABC Computers. <u>Do you know</u> our company?
B <u>Yes, I do</u>. You <u>sell</u> software.
A That's right.
B Well, I'm the new manager of the computer department. Chloe Lester.
A How do you do. I'm Michael Harper.
B Good to meet you, Michael. Do you know Sara Cooper?
A No, I <u>don't know</u> her.
B She works for ABC, too.
A It's a big company.

2 Complete the questions and answers.

1 Q: Where .... Claire work?   A: She .... in Manchester.
2 Q: .... Chloe know his company?   A: Yes, she ....
3 Q: What .... his company sell?   A: It .... software.
4 Q: .... Michael know Sara Cooper?   A: No, he ....
5 Q: Which company .... Sara work for?   A: She .... for ABC Computers.

Reading

A police officer

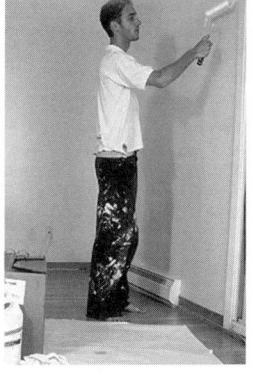
B painter

C mechanic

Who are these sentences about? You decide. Some of the sentences are true for two people. Write A for the police officer, B for the painter, and C for the mechanic.

1 He wears a uniform.
2 He doesn't wear a uniform.
3 He works at weekends.
4 He works alone.
5 He works in a garage.
6 He doesn't work for a company.
7 He travels in his job.
8 He doesn't travel in his job.
9 He works inside.
10 He does a dangerous job.
11 He wears overalls.
12 He doesn't work regular hours.
13 He meets a lot of people.
14 He hasn't got any qualifications.
15 He works with a partner.
16 He works in the same place every day.
17 He wears old jeans at work.
18 He works for a company.
19 Sometimes he works at night.
20 He works from Monday to Saturday lunchtime.

The next word

Put a cross (X) by any words that don't go with the words in bold.

- **I work** ✓ from 9 to 5   ✓ on Saturdays   ✗ manager   ✓ in a bank

He works ☐ for IBM   ☐ part-time   ☐ retired   ☐ regular hours   ☐ full-time

I know ☐ them   ☐ him   ☐ the answer   ☐ us   ☐ her phone number

She's ☐ a student   ☐ unemployed   ☐ retired   ☐ work in a shop

It sells ☐ salesperson   ☐ software   ☐ bicycles   ☐ on the Internet   ☐ aspirins

I've got ☐ a job   ☐ a degree   ☐ a headache   ☐ brown eyes   ☐ at university

seven

Grammar

1   **Complete the table with these words.**

    Are   some   Is   an   any   a

Positive and negative			
There	is	.....	airport.
	isn't	.....	railway station.
	are	.....	museums.
	aren't	.....	factories.

Questions			
.....	there	a	university?
.....		any	pubs?

2   **Tick (✓) the correct words.**
1   (☐ It ☐ There) 's a car park in the town centre.
2   There aren't (☐ any ☐ some) mountains near the city.
3   The town hasn't got (☐ many ☐ some) hotels.
4   What's that place? (☐ There ☐ It)'s the new art gallery.
5   There (☐ is ☐ are) three cinemas in the town.
6   What's the population? (☐ There are ☐ It is) about 250,000.
7   There isn't (☐ a ☐ any) cathedral in the city.

Articles: *a / an, the,* 'zero' article

Complete with *a, an, the,* or (–) for no article.

Liam lives in ..... Dublin, the capital of ..... Ireland. He lives near ..... city centre, and his house is near ..... River Liffey. He lives in ..... old, eighteenth-century house. There's ..... pub next door. Liam is ..... student. He lives with his parents. His mother works in ..... hospital, and his father is ..... architect.

Using your dictionary: plurals

> **country** /ˈkʌntri/ *noun*
> **1** (*plural* **countries**) an area of land with its own people and government: *France, Spain and Portugal are countries.*
> **2 the country** (no plural) land that is not in a town: *Do you live in the town or the country?*

Find the plurals of these words.

beach   art gallery   university   boy   city   theatre   address

Writing: capital letters

1 Look at the rules and the examples. Add extra examples in column 3.

	Rule	Example	Extra examples
1	At the beginning of a sentence	We live in the country. He's my friend.	....
2	Names of people or groups	Joseph Smith The Rolling Stones	....
3	Titles of people	Mr, Dr	....
4	Cities and countries	Belfast, Ireland	....
5	Geographical names	Lake Michigan Mount Kilimanjaro	....
6	Days and months	Monday, January	....
7	Companies and organizations	Apple Computers Arsenal FC	....
8	Abbreviations	BBC, CIA	....
9	Titles of books, films, CDs	*The Lord of the Rings*	....
10	I (subject pronoun)	Where am I?	....

2 Write the paragraph with capital letters.

liverpool is a city in the county of lancashire in england. the city is on the river mersey and was famous in the 1960s for the music of the beatles. there are two famous football teams in the city, liverpool and everton. the old docks are now a tourist attraction. there are two art galleries, the walker art gallery and the tate gallery. liverpool has two cathedrals. the airport is seven miles from the city, and it is called john lennon airport after the beatle, who was murdered in 1980.

eight

Time

Complete.

Analogue	Digital	Analogue	Digital
	twelve hundred		nine thirty
	eleven five		six thirty-five
ten past eight		twenty to one	
quarter past four			ten forty-five
	seven twenty	ten to five	
twenty-five past two			eight fifty-five

Arrivals and departures

Match these sentences to the cartoons.
Write the letters A to F in the speech bubbles.

A How long does it take to Alpha Centauri?
B The time in London is twelve noon. The time at our destination is twelve midnight. Please change your watches now.
C When do we arrive in Rome?
D What time do we get to Dodge City?
E Does this bus stop at the railway station?
F When does the next train leave?

Find the information

1 What time does Flight 4319 arrive in Singapore? ....
2 What time does Flight 024 leave Singapore? ....
3 When does Flight 024 get to Auckland? ....
4 How long does the flight from Auckland to Los Angeles take? ....
5 Does the flight from Los Angeles to London stop anywhere? ....

www.flybywire.com

Book online | **Timetables** | **Fares** | **Contact us**

**** SPECIAL 'Round the World' PRICE ****

Trip summary

Departure from
UK
LONDON

Destination
NEW ZEALAND
AUCKLAND

Departure date
14 Oct

Return date
11 Nov

Price
Lowest
economy

GO

DEPARTING FLIGHTS via Singapore

	DEPARTS	ARRIVES	
Air New Zealand Flight 4319 (operated by Singapore Airlines)	LONDON 14 October 21.05	SINGAPORE 15 October 16.50 (next day)	Non-stop 10881 km Boeing 747 11 hours 45 min Connect to ▶
Air New Zealand Flight 024	DEPARTS SINGAPORE 15 October 20.20	ARRIVES AUCKLAND 16 October 11.10 (2nd day)	Non-stop 8408 km Boeing 767 10 hours 50 min

RETURN FLIGHTS via Los Angeles

	DEPARTS	ARRIVES	
Air New Zealand Flight 9842 (operated by United Airlines)	AUCKLAND 11 November 18.30	LOS ANGELES 11 November 09.30 (across International Date Line)	Non-stop 10461 km Boeing 777 11 hours 0 min Connect to ▶
Air New Zealand Flight 002	DEPARTS LOS ANGELES 11 November 14.45	ARRIVES LONDON 12 November 09.10 (Next day)	Non-stop 8778 km Boeing 747 10 hours 25 min

get

Make sentences. Add more examples.

You can get	money	outside the airport terminal.
	a taxi	at the coffee shop.
	a cup of tea	from the cash machine.

What time	do you	get	to work?
When	does it		home in the evening?
			to London?

nine

Grammar: pronouns

subject pronoun	I	you	he	she	it	we	they
object pronoun	.....	.....	.....	.....	.....	.....	.....

Complete the table with the <u>underlined</u> words from these sentences.

1 Do you know <u>them</u>?
2 Don't forget. Send <u>us</u> a postcard.
3 Is it for <u>him</u> or for <u>her</u>?
4 Phone <u>me</u> at six o'clock.
5 Turn <u>it</u> off!
6 Happy birthday! This is for <u>you</u>.

Reading: signs

Read the signs and find words which mean:

Look right and left   Be careful   area   24 hours

Imperatives

1 **Complete the sentences with these words. Be careful with capital letters!**

   turn off   come in   don't forget   turn on
   watch out   help me

1 ...., please sit down.
2 Please .... with my homework.
3 There's a good programme on BBC1. .... the TV.
4 ....! There's a dog on the road!
5 Please .... all mobile phones.
6 ...., it's her birthday next week.

2 Do these things.

1 Print your name in BLOCK CAPITALS. ....
2 Then underline your first name.
3 Put a circle round your family name.
4 Are you male or female? Tick the box   M ☐   F ☐.
5 Sign your name on the dotted line.   ....

Prepositions

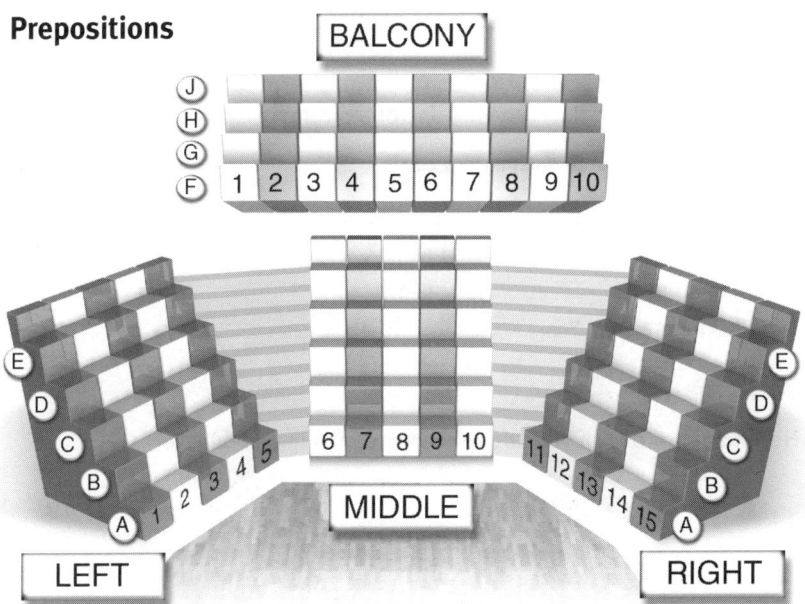

1 **Where are these seats?**

E2   A8   D7   H4   C8   B14   B6

1 Which seat is at the front in the middle?
2 Which seat is at the back on the left?
3 Which seat is on the right, near the front?
4 Which seat is in the middle?
5 Which seat is in the balcony?
6 Which seat is in the middle of row C?
7 Which seat is on the left of the middle section?

2 **Make sentences about these seats.**

C10   E15   F5   J1   E8   D5   A14   G10

- *C10 is on the right of the middle section.*

ten

Grammar: *can / can't*

1 Tick (✓) the correct words.
1. She can't (☐ speak ☐ to speak ☐ speaking) Italian.
2. (☐ Does he can ☐ Is he can ☐ Can he) play chess?
3. We (☐ don't can ☐ aren't can ☐ can't) go to the party.
4. Can you help me? Sorry, I (☐ don't ☐ can't ☐ 'm cannot).
5. (☐ Can ☐ Am ☐ Do) I see the doctor tomorrow, please?

2 Complete the table with *can* or *can't*.

Positive	I .... play the guitar.
Negative	He .... drive.
Questions	.... you swim?
Short answers	Yes, I .... No, I ....

Word map

How many words can you add to the word map in one minute?

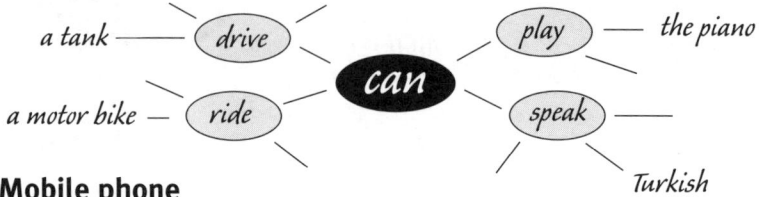

Mobile phone

1 Complete.

> Hello? Yes? Speak up. I .... hear you.
> I'm on the .... to London now. (...)
> It arrives .... 10.35. Can you
> meet .... ? (...)
> You can't? Oh, dear. Why .... ? (...)
> Well, that's OK. I can get .... taxi.
> How long does it .... from the
> station .... your place? (...)
> Forty minutes? Oh, dear. That ....
> expensive in a taxi. .... I get an
> underground train? (...)
> Good. See .... about eleven thirty.
> Bye then. (...) Yes, bye. (...) Bye. (...)

2 What is the other person saying (...)? Can you guess?

Abilities

Are these sentences true or false? Do you know? If not, can you guess? The answers are in the key.

1 A female grey parrot in New York can say 555 words.
2 Parrots can speak, but they can't understand.
3 Elephants can't swim.
4 Elephants can live for one hundred years.
5 Dolphins can swim at 50 kilometres an hour.
6 Dolphins can learn to speak English. 
7 Cats can see in the dark.
8 Cats can live for more than 30 years.
9 Gorillas can communicate in sign language.
10 Gorillas can grow to two metres tall.
11 Swans can swim, but they can't fly.
12 One kind of swan can fly at 8,000 metres.

Writing: contractions

We don't use contractions in formal English.

Write the full forms of these contractions.

1 I'm not   ....   5 He's got   ....
2 She's not ....   6 I don't   ....
3 We're not ....   7 It doesn't ....
4 I've got   ....   8 I can't   ....

eleven

Grammar: countable and uncountable

Countable					
positive	There	are	some	.....	in the car.
negative		aren't	any	.....	on the plate.
questions	Are	there		.....	on the answerphone?

Uncountable					
positive	There	is	some	.....	in the glass.
negative		isn't	any	.....	on the plate.
questions	Is	there		.....	in the car?

1 **Complete the table with these words.**

   people   chips   milk   messages   rice   petrol

2 **Are these words countable or uncountable? Write C or U.**
   1 yogurt ☐   6 eggs ☐   11 grapes ☐   16 slices of bread ☐
   2 beans ☐   7 water ☐   12 vegetables ☐   17 butter ☐
   3 food ☐   8 nuts ☐   13 flour ☐   18 litres of water ☐
   4 meat ☐   9 bread ☐   14 chocolate ☐   19 soup ☐
   5 salad ☐   10 sugar ☐   15 chocolates ☐   20 cans of beer ☐

3 **These words aren't in the Student's Book unit. Can you guess if they are countable or uncountable? Write C or U.**

coins, Canadian dollars

notes (UK), bills (US), Australian dollars

money, Canadian money

paper

magazines

coal

onions

onion

onion rings

Possessive 's

1 Apostrophe + s ('s) is missing from these sentences. Add it in the correct place.

- She's got some new trainers.   *has*

1 There some water in the glass.   ....
2 Is that Sarah car?   ....
3 St James Palace is in London.   ....
4 Michael got some salad on his plate.   ....
5 Whose cup this?   ....
6 Do you know Paul sister?   ....
7 Anna got a new boyfriend.   ....
8 Where Sandra?   ....

2 What does 's mean in the sentences? Write *is*, *has*, or *possessive*.

Quiz

1 Complete the quiz with these question words.

> Where   What   When   Who   Which   How old

2 Underline the possessive examples.

3 Do the quiz. The answers are in the key.

1 .... is Michaelangelo's *David*?
   ☐ about 500 years ☐ about 2,000 years ☐ about 100 years

2 .... is Saudi Arabia's chief export?
   ☐ rice ☐ oil ☐ aluminium

3 .... English city is The Beatles's home town?
   ☐ London ☐ Manchester ☐ Liverpool

4 .... is Microsoft's head office?
   ☐ Seattle, USA ☐ London, UK
   ☐ Vancouver, Canada

5 .... is Prince Charles's mother?
   ☐ Queen Victoria ☐ Queen Mary
   ☐ Queen Elizabeth

6 .... is St. Valentine's Day?
   ☐ 1st April ☐ 14th February
   ☐ 25th December

twelve

Grammar: would like

1 Put the words in the correct order to make sentences.
- tea? / you / some / like / Would   *Would you like some tea?*
1. tickets / like? / many / you / would / How
2. one / I'd / another /please. / like
3. ice / like? / much / you / How / would
4. please. / these / I'd / some / like / of
5. one / would / like? / she / Which

2 Complete the sentences with *would*, *wouldn't*, or *'d*.

request	I .... like some milk.
offer	.... you like some lemon?
short answers	Yes, I .... Yes, please.
	No, I .... No, thanks.

Responses

Match the questions and answers.

1. Would you like some ice?
2. Have you got any ice?
3. What would you like to drink?
4. Which one would you like?
5. Which ones would you like?
6. Which is David's book?

A Tea, please.
B The chocolate one.
C The chocolate ones.
D Sorry, we haven't.
E It's the blue one.
F Yes, please.

Countable / uncountable

Tick (✓) the correct word.

1. How many (☐ biscuits ☐ tea) would you like?
2. How (☐ many ☐ much) oranges are there?
3. How (☐ many ☐ much) milk is there?
4. How much (☐ time ☐ hours) have you got?
5. How much (☐ water ☐ peas) would you like?
6. How much petrol (☐ is ☐ are) there?
7. How many seats (☐ is ☐ are) there?
8. Where (☐ do ☐ does) rice come from?
9. Where (☐ do ☐ does) bananas come from?
10. Would you like (☐ a ☐ some) cup of coffee?

UNIT TWELVE

How many?

1 Make questions with *How many?*

- Q: *How many states are there in the USA?*
  A: There are (☐ 48   ☐ 50   ☐ 51) states in the USA.

1 Q: ....
   A: There are (☐ 24   ☐ 26   ☐ 28) letters in the English alphabet.

2 Q: ....
   A: There are (☐ 9   ☐ 11   ☐ 12) players in a baseball team.

3 Q: ....
   A: There are (☐ 1.2   ☐ 1.6   ☐ 6.1) kilometres in a mile.

4 Q: ....
   A: There are (☐ 120   ☐ 240   ☐ 360) degrees (°) in a circle.

2 Choose the correct answers. Check with the answer key.

How much?

1 Make questions with *How much?*

- Q: *How much of an iceberg is underwater?*
  A: (☐ 50%   ☐ 60%   ☐ 80%) of an iceberg is under water.

1 Q: ....
   A: (☐ 49%   ☐ 71%   ☐ 76%) of the Earth's surface is water.

2 Q: ....
   A: About (☐ 12%   ☐ 17%   ☐ 23%) of the land on the Earth is desert.

3 Q: ....
   A: About (☐ 3%   ☐ 10%   ☐ 13%) of the land on the Earth is under ice.

5 Q: ....
   A: (☐ 25%   ☐ 50%   ☐ 70%) of the human body is water.

2 Choose the correct answers. Check with the answer key.

thirteen

Symbols

Label the signs with these words.

escalator   coffee shop   bar   car park   telephone   lift
information   cashpoint   toilets   restaurant

1..........   2..........   3..........   4..........   5..........
6..........   7..........   8..........   9..........   10..........

Responses

Match the questions and answers.

1 Is it far?
2 How long does it take?
3 Can I help you?
4 What floor is it on?
5 Is this Bond Street?
6 Where's the coffee shop?
7 Are you finding everything OK?

A No, thanks. I'm just looking.
B The second.
C Sorry, I'm a stranger. I don't know.
D No, it's only about 400 metres.
E It's over there, next to Reception.
F Yes, I am. Thank you.
G About ten minutes.

Asking for help

Tick (✓) the correct words.

A Excuse me, I'm (☐ looking ☐ trying) to find London Street.
B London Street? OK, go (☐ along ☐ past) this road to the (☐ end ☐ stop), and turn right. That's Bath Road. Go along Bath Road, and go past the Town Hall. London Street is the (☐ third ☐ three) on (☐ a ☐ the) left. You can't (☐ turn ☐ miss) it. (☐ There's ☐ There are) a NatWest Bank on the corner.
A Thank you. Is it very (☐ far ☐ distance)?
B No, (☐ not ☐ no) far. You can walk there (☐ of ☐ in) about ten minutes.

Directions

Hotel plan

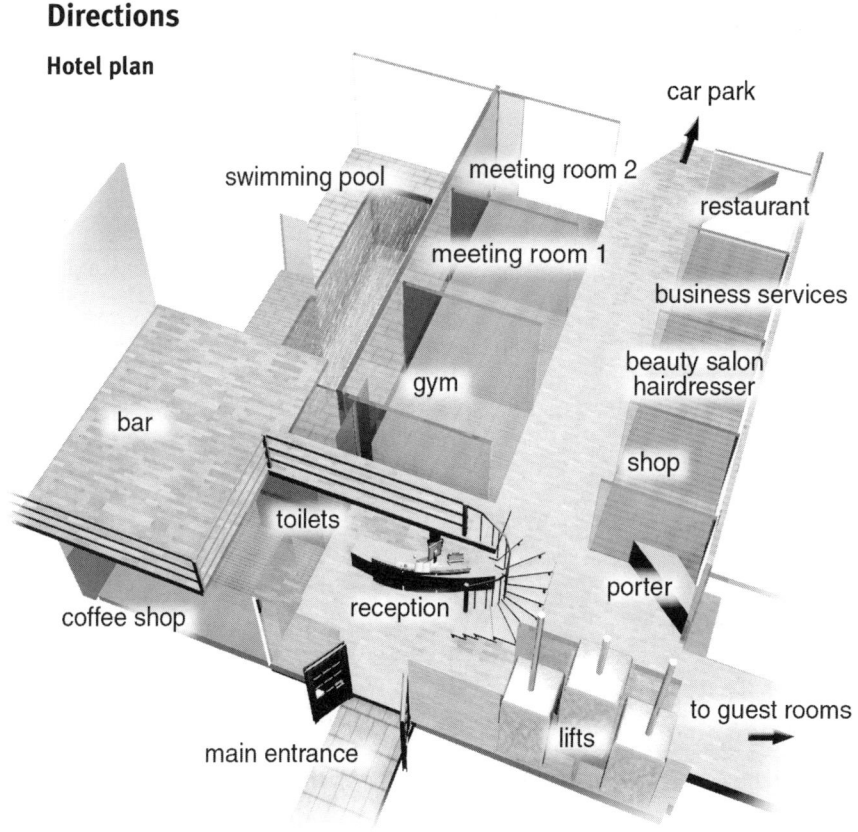

1 **Look at the plan. Complete the spaces with these words.**

past   left   next   along   upstairs   second

A **You are at reception. You're looking for meeting room 1.**

Receptionist: OK, turn .... at the stairs and go .... the corridor.

It's the .... door on the ....

B **You are in the coffee shop. You're looking for the bar.**

Waiter: Go .... reception. There are some stairs .... to

reception. Go .... That's the bar.

2 **Give directions:**
1 from the coffee shop to business services.
2 from the car park to the gym.
3 from the lifts to meeting room 2.
4 from the coffee shop to the beauty salon.

fourteen

Grammar: present continuous

Positive and negative		
subject pronoun	auxiliary verb	main verb
I	.....	working.
	am	reading.
	'm not	listening.
You	.....	doing it.
We	are	driving.
They	aren't	
He	.....	
She	is	
It	.....	

Questions		
auxiliary verb	subject pronoun	main verb
Am	I	working?
		reading?
		listening?
.....	.....	doing it?
	we	driving?
	.....	
.....	.....	
	she	
	it	

Short answers	
Yes, I am.	No, I'm not.
Yes, (you) are.	.....
Yes, he is.	No, (she) isn't.

Read the conversation. Complete the table with the underlined words.

A Hi. What <u>are you</u> doing?
B <u>I'm</u> reading an e-mail from my brother.
A Lee? Where <u>is he</u> working now?
B He <u>isn't</u> working.
  He<u>'s</u> having a long holiday in the USA.
A Where's he staying?
B Different places. He's with Sarah.
  They<u>'re</u> travelling across the USA.
A Are <u>they</u> driving?
B <u>No, they aren't</u>. They're travelling by bus.

Responses

Match the questions and answers.

1 Who are you phoning?   A Home. I'm tired.
2 What are you doing?   B Liverpool. Three nil. It's a great game.
3 What are you reading?   C My sister.
4 Where are you going?   D I'm waiting for a phone call.
5 Who's winning?   E He's sitting next to Sarah. The tall man.
6 Which one's Mark?   F *Lord of The Rings*. It's very long.

Christmas Day

1 Read the text and put the names in the boxes.

In Australia, December 25th is in the middle of the summer, but people have a traditional English Christmas dinner of turkey. The Cook family are having dinner together. They're sitting on the patio. Paul Cook is eating. His daughter, Jessica, is taking a photo of her brother, Jake. Jake's holding a surfboard. Jessica's boyfriend, Dylan, is standing and drinking from a can of beer. Paul's other daughter, Jodie, is pouring a glass of water. Fiona Scott's holding a glass of wine and she's talking to Jake.

2 Complete the questions and answers.

1. Q: What .... eating? A: They're .... turkey.
2. Q: Where are they .... ? A: .... sitting .... the patio.
3. Q: Who's .... a photo? A: .... is.
4. Q: Who's .... a surfboard? A: Jake ....
5. Q: What .... Dylan doing? A: .... drinking.
6. Q: Who's .... a glass of water? A: Jodie ....
7. Q: Who .... Fiona .... to? A: .... talking .... Jake.

fifteen

Grammar: likes and dislikes

Positive and negative		
I	like	tea.
They	don't like	swimming.
She	likes	
He	doesn't like	

Questions			
Do	you	like	tea?
	they		swimming?
Does	she		

Requests		
I	'd like	tea.
She	wouldn't like	some tea.

Offers			
Would	you	like	tea?
	she		some tea?

1 Where can you add these words to the tables?

watching TV   some beer   tennis   coffee   dancing

2 Tick (✓) the correct words.

Sue (☐ Do ☐ Would) you like football?
Ben Yes, I love it.
Sue Do you (☐ playing ☐ play) football?
Ben No, (☐ I don't ☐ I'm not). But I love (☐ go ☐ going) to football matches, and I like (☐ watch ☐ watching) it on TV.
Sue Which is your favourite team?
Ben Manchester United, of course. What about you?
Sue (☐ I ☐ I'd) love football too. (☐ I'd play ☐ I play) every Saturday.
Ben What?
Sue Yes, (☐ I'd play ☐ I play) for a women's team. I'm a striker.

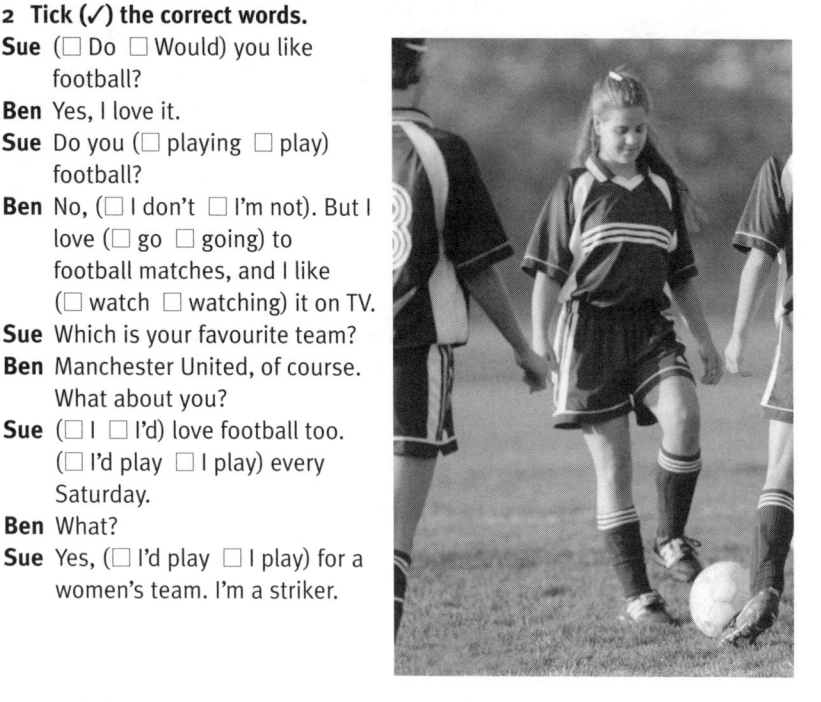

3 Tick (✓) the correct words.

He (☐ loves ☐ is loving) football, but he (☐ don't ☐ doesn't) play it. He (☐ like ☐ likes) (☐ go ☐ going) to football matches and (☐ watch ☐ watching) it on TV. She (☐ is loving ☐ loves) football too, and she (☐ would play ☐ plays) for a women's team.

like, would like, love

Complete the sentences with the correct form of *like*, *would like*, or *love*.

[Panel 1: YOUR TIE! / OH, THANK YOU.]
[Panel 2: TEA OR COFFEE? / COFFEE, PLEASE.]
[Panel 3: WHAT ___ DOING IN YOUR FREE TIME? / SHOPPING.]
[Panel 4: ___ A CHEESEBURGER, PLEASE. / AND WOULD YOU LIKE KETCHUP ON THAT?]
[Panel 5: CLASSICAL MUSIC? / NO, I HATE IT.]
[Panel 6: ME? / ME?]

The next word

Put a cross (✗) by any words that don't go with the words in bold.

- **I love**   ✓ him   ✓ your dress   ✗ cook   ✓ swimming

Would you like ...? ☐ another drink   ☐ playing chess   ☐ some milk
☐ anything else

Do you like ...? ☐ anything else   ☐ shopping   ☐ strawberries   ☐ them

Can you ...? ☐ type   ☐ play the piano   ☐ help me   ☐ driving

I hate   ☐ you   ☐ doing housework   ☐ tomatoes   ☐ speak in class

I'm   ☐ work   ☐ doing homework   ☐ twenty-five   ☐ tired

sixteen

Grammar

function	grammar	examples
Arrangements	Present continuous + future time word	☐ ☐
Talking about the future	*be + going to* + bare infinitive (you can add a time word)	☐ ☐
Future intentions	*be + going to* + bare infinitive (you can add a time word)	☐ ☐
Suggestions	*Let's* + bare infinitive *What / How + about + -ing* form	☐ ☐

Put these example sentences in the table.
1 I'm going to be a police officer.
2 I'm seeing the doctor tomorrow.
3 The bus is going to be late.
4 We're going to the beach on Sunday.
5 Let's meet at ten fifteen.
6 It's going to rain.
7 I'm going to buy a new jacket.
8 How about going for a drink?

The next word

Put a cross (✗) by any words that don't go with the words in bold.
- **I'm going to** ✓ study French   ✓ be a doctor   ✗ learning English   ✓ leave school

Let's ☐ go   ☐ going to the cinema   ☐ meet at ten   ☐ have a drink
How about ...? ☐ going to a club   ☐ another drink   ☐ Friday   ☐ go home
I'm going to ☐ studying   ☐ be a teacher   ☐ Bristol University   ☐ watch TV
I'm meeting him ☐ tomorrow   ☐ at six thirty   ☐ at the station   ☐ often
It's going to ☐ rain   ☐ be hot   ☐ snowing   ☐ thunder

Question words

Complete the questions with these question words.

What time   Which   How much   Where   What   How many   How long

1 '.......... are you going to stay?' 'In a hotel.'
2 '.......... are you meeting her?' 'Eight o'clock.'
3 '.......... is it going to take?' 'About two hours.'
4 '.......... are you going to wear?' 'My new jeans.'
5 '.......... money are you going to spend?' 'A lot!'
6 '.......... people are coming to the party?' 'About twenty.'
7 '.......... team is going to win?' 'I don't know.'

Reading

Lucy   Andy   Malik   Nadine   Becky   Rob

These British students are eighteen. They're taking their exams in June, and they're leaving school after the exams.
- Two of them are going to take a 'gap year' before university.
- Two of them are going to start work.
- Two of them are going to study in the autumn.

> **gap** / gæp / noun **1** a space between two things or in the middle of something. *Leave a gap between your car and the next. There's a gap in the wall.* **2** a space where something is missing. *Complete the gaps in the sentences.* **3** a period of time when something stops, or between two events. *They stopped speaking. There was a gap in the conversation. They met after a gap of ten years.* (Br.E) a gap year (= a year between school and university when some students work to earn money, or travel) **4** a difference that separates people or things: the gap between the rich and poor. *There's a gap in the market* (= business opportunity).

1 Read, then match the sentences to the students.
1. 'I've got a place at university for October next year. I love travelling, so I'm going to backpack round the world first.'
2. 'I've got a job in an office. I'm leaving school on June 21st. I'm starting work on June 24th.'
3. 'I'm going to Bath University in October this year. I'm going to study Physics and Astronomy.'
4. 'I'm going to do voluntary work for a year before university. I'm going to work in a school. I like working with small children.'
5. 'I'm not going to go to university. I don't like studying. I'm looking for a job at the moment.'
6. 'I've got a summer job, then I'm going to do kung-fu in China. I'm going to be a martial arts teacher.'

2 Think about your answers. Can you guess from people's appearance (what they look like)? Really, you don't know!

seventeen

Grammar: past simple *be*

1 Complete the table.

Positive and negative		
I, He, She, It	was	here.
	.....	at school.
We, You, They	.....	tired.
	weren't	

Questions		
Was	I, he, she, it	there?
Were	we, you, they	at school?
		tired?

Short answers			
Yes, (I)	No, (he)	Yes, (we)	No, (we) ......

2 Put the words in the correct order to make sentences.

- you / school / yesterday? / Were / at
  Were you at school yesterday?

1 night. / at / weren't / last / We / home
2 in / She / born / Canada. / was
3 office / He / yesterday. / his / wasn't / in
4 Saturday / you / Where / evening? / last / were
5 at / She / asleep / o'clock / night. / was / ten / last
6 were / children / noisy. / The / very

Twentieth-century faces

1 Complete the sentences with *was, wasn't,* or *were*.

1 Three of them .... born in the USA.

2 Two of them .... born in Britain. One of them .... born in Britain, but she .... born in England.

Bruce Lee 1940–1973 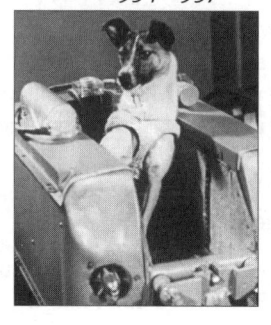 *Laika 1954–1957*  *J.R.R. Tolkien 1892–1973*

3 One of them .... Chinese, but he .... born in China. He .... born in San Francisco, but he .... first famous in Hong Kong.

4 One of them .... Argentinian.

5 One of them .... Russian. It .... born about 1954.

2 Quiz. Do you know the answers to these questions? Check your answers in the key.

1 Which two were the wives of presidents?
2 Which one was the wife of a king?
3 Which one was born in the nineteenth century?
4 Which one was alive in the twenty-first century?
5 Which one was the first animal in space?
6 Which one was a writer and an Oxford professor?
7 Which two were actors?
8 Which one was born in Scotland?
9 Which one was famous for martial arts?
10 Which two were British?
11 Which one was the subject of the musical *Evita*?
12 Which two were politicians?
13 Which two were born in 1919?
14 Which one was over 100 years old?

3 Write two questions and answers.
- Q: *When was Bruce Lee born?* A: *He was born in 1940.*

Dates

5/11/03
In British English this is 5th November 2003 (day/month/year).
In American English this is May 11th 2003 (month/day/year).

What are these dates in (a) British English and (b) American English?

1/12/05   2/10/96   3/9/04   4/6/00   5/8/99   11/7/06

Queen Elizabeth,
The Queen Mother
1900–2002

John F. Kennedy 1917–1963
Jacqueline Kennedy
1919–1994

Eva Perón 1919–1952

eighteen

Grammar: past simple – irregular verbs

1 Complete the table.

Subject pronoun	Positive	Negative
I, You, He, She, It, We, They	went	didn't .....
	.....	didn't have
	saw	..... see

Questions	Short answers
..... (you) go?	Yes, (I) did.
Did (he) .....?	No, (they) .....
Did (they) see?	

2 Complete the table with past tense verbs.

present	past	present	past	present	past
am / is	was	don't / doesn't	didn't	go	
am / is not		have		see	
are	were	buy		come	came
aren't		get		know	knew
do / does		fly			

3 Match the first question with a second question.

1 Did you go to a bank yesterday? A Who did you go out with?
2 Did you go for a walk yesterday? B How much money did you get?
3 Did you go to a restaurant yesterday? C Which film did you see?
4 Did you go to the cinema yesterday? D Where did you go?
5 Did you go out with a friend yesterday? E What did you eat?

The next word

Put a cross (X) by any words that don't go with the words in bold.

- **I had** ✓ a bath X tired ✓ a headache ✓ breakfast ✓ a shower

It was ☐ hot ☐ cloudy ☐ sunny ☐ be cold ☐ lovely
We went ☐ home ☐ to the mall ☐ got ☐ out ☐ in
She saw ☐ he ☐ us ☐ a good film ☐ something ☐ that
They were ☐ late ☐ on time ☐ departure ☐ there ☐ early
He bought ☐ it ☐ some milk ☐ happy ☐ a DVD ☐ a lot

Shopping lists

1 What do people write most often? Is it postcards? Letters? e-mails?
It's not any of these! The answer is shopping lists.
Look at Cathy's shopping list. What is she going to buy?
Think of sentences.

- *She's going to buy some fruit.*

fruit
vegetables
milk
bread
brown sauce
pizza x2
salad
biscuits
cooking oil
coffee
yogurt

Safebury's
Oxbridge 3 0(1156) 789600
VAT NO. 000 456 789 21
www.safebury.co.uk

```
FRESH MILK SEMI-SKIMMED     0.92
PIZZA MARGHERITA S/B        3.99
PIZZA MARGHERITA S/B        3.99
4 LEAF SALAD                2.09
STRAWBERRY YOGURT x 6       2.99
H.P. SAUCE                  1.49
HEINZ TOMATO KETCHUP        1.75
ITALIAN OLIVE OIL 500 ML    5.99
WHITE FRENCH BREAD          1.69
BANANAS JAMAICA 0.97Kg      1.71
RED GRAPES U.S.A. 0.62Kg    2.83
MIXED VEGETABLE PKT         2.79
NEW POTATOES 0.5 Kg         1.85
ORGANIC TOMATOES UK         2.35
PARMESAN CHEESE 0.21Kg      4.21
CHOC COOKIES CADBURY        1.99

16 ITEMS PURCHASED
TOTAL DUE                  42.63
MASTERCARD                 42.63
CHANGE DUE                  0.00
DATE: 31 AUG TIME: 15.03
CASHIER: 2486
```

Thank you for shopping at Safebury's

2 Look at the till receipt from the supermarket.
1 What fruit did Cathy buy?
2 What vegetables did she buy?
3 Which item did she forget from her list? (*got* is the past tense of *get*. Guess the past tense of *forget*.)
4 Which extra things did she buy?

3 Look at the receipt again.
Find the answers.
1 Where was the olive oil from?
2 Where were the bananas from?
3 What colour were the grapes?
4 What flavour were the yogurts?

Writing

Write a shopping list for yourself in English. Write more than ten items on your list.
Use these categories:
   Fruit Vegetables Meat / Fish
   Dairy products Other items

nineteen

Grammar and spelling: regular verbs

Change these regular verbs to the past tense, then put the verbs in the correct columns.

die	marry	divorce	play	move	want	study	phone	travel
stop	like	hate	start	live	reply	stay		

+ -ed	+ -d	-y + -ed	-y ➡ -ied	double letter + -ed
…………	…………	…………	…………	…………
…………	…………	…………	…………	…………
…………	…………	…………	…………	…………

Reading: a biography

Lord of the Dance

Michael Flatley was born in Chicago on 16 July 1958. He was the second of five children. His parents were Irish immigrants, and his mother and grandmother were champion Irish dancers. Michael went to Ireland every summer. He's American, but he speaks with an Irish accent. He started dancing when he was eleven. He won the All-World Irish Dancing Championship when he was seventeen. In the 1990s he moved to California, and toured the world with the traditional Irish music group, The Chieftains.

He created 'Riverdance' in 1994 for the Eurovision Song Contest in Dublin, and became a star overnight. He directed and starred in 'Lord of the Dance' in 1997 and the video sold three million copies. In 2000, four million people in Europe saw his show 'Feet of Flames'. In the USA, he danced at New York's Madison Square Garden, which was his dream of a lifetime. He retired after his final show in Dallas, Texas in July 2001.

1 Read the text. Complete the table with past tense verbs.

present	past	present	past	present	past
become		create		win	
dance		direct		tour	
go		move		start	
retire		see			
sell		star			

2 Find these things.
1 Michael's date of birth
2 the titles of three dance shows
3 three American cities
4 one Irish city
5 two American states
6 the name of a music group

3 Answer these questions.
1 What happened every summer when he was young?
2 What happened when he was eleven?
3 What happened when he was seventeen?
4 What happened in 1994?
5 What happened in July 2001?

Connecting: *and / but*

He was born in America <u>but</u> he speaks with an Irish accent.
He directed <u>and</u> starred in 'Lord of The Dance'.

Now choose the correct words, *and* or *but*.
1 I was born in Singapore, (and / but) I went to school in England.
2 I was born (and / but) went to school in Nigeria.
3 I started university in 2000 (and / but) finished in 2003.
4 I like dancing (and / but) I'm not a good dancer.
5 I studied French (and / but) I can't speak it very well.
6 I work in an office (and / but) I like my job.

Writing: autobiography

1 Think about these questions.
Where were you born?
Where did you go to school?
What did you do in the summer when you were young?
When did you start school / college / work?
What do you do now?

2 Then write a short autobiography (a biography of yourself).
Don't write more than ten sentences. Try to connect some sentences with *and* and *but*.

twenty

Grammar: subject and object questions
Elvis married Priscilla.
Elvis is the **subject** of the sentence.
Priscilla is the **object** of the sentence.

Elvis bought a Cadillac.
Elvis is the **subject** of the sentence.
A Cadillac is the **object** of the sentence.

Subject question
We want information about the subject, *Elvis*.
Who **married** Priscilla? Elvis did. / Elvis married Priscilla.
Who **bought** a Cadillac? Elvis did. / Elvis bought a Cadillac.

Object question
We want information about the object, *Priscilla* or a *Cadillac*.
Who **did** Elvis **marry**? Priscilla. / He married Priscilla.
What **did** Elvis **buy**? A Cadillac. / He bought a Cadillac.

Write a subject question and an object question for these sentences.

	sentence	subject question	object question
1	John phoned Jacqui.		
2	Anna forgot her book.		
3	Sarah brought the wine.		
4	Angela kissed Tony.		
5	Zoe interviewed Shaun.		
6	Chris carried the shopping.		

Past tenses

Complete the table with past tense verbs.

present	past	present	past	present	past
bring		carry		put	
come		draw		run	
fall		forget		take	
give		pay		think	
hold				write	

History

1 Match the start of a sentence (1 to 10) to the end of a sentence (A to J).

1. Leonardo da Vinci (paint)
2. Princess Diana (die)
3. Neil Armstrong (go)
4. World War II (end)
5. The Berlin Wall (fall)
6. Shakespeare (live)
7. Vivaldi (write)
8. Bill Gates (start)
9. Matt Groening (create)
10. The Wright Brothers (fly)

A in 1989.
B to the Moon in 1969.
C in England.
D *The Four Seasons*.
E Microsoft.
F the *Mona Lisa*.
G 'The Simpsons' TV series.
H the first plane in 1903.
I in a car crash.
J in 1945.

2 Put the verb in brackets in the past tense. Write the sentence.

- *Leonardo da Vinci painted the* Mona Lisa.

3 Complete the sentences with the question words.

How   What   Where   Which   Who   When

1. .... painted the *Mona Lisa*?
2. .... did Princess Diana die?
3. .... did Neil Armstrong go?
4. .... did World War II end?
5. .... fell in 1989?
6. .... did Shakespeare live?
7. .... wrote *The Four Seasons*?
8. .... company did Bill Gates start?
9. .... created The Simpsons?
10. .... did the Wright Brothers do in 1903?

4 Look at questions 1, 7, and 9. They are subject questions. Make object questions with *What* about the same event.

twenty-one

Grammar: frequency adverbs

1 Put the frequency adverbs on the diagram.

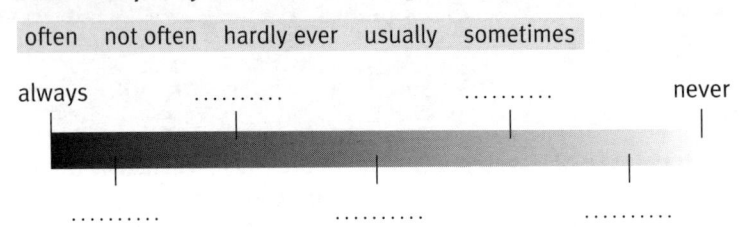

often   not often   hardly ever   usually   sometimes

always .... never

....

Frequency adverbs go before the main verb.
Frequency adverbs go after the auxiliary verb.

	auxiliary verb	frequency adverb	main verb	
They	are	often		late.
We	don't	often	watch	TV.
You		often	play	tennis.

2 Put the words in the correct order to make sentences.

- at / I / o'clock. / usually / seven / get up
  I usually get up at seven o'clock.
1. late. / never / are / They
2. fish. / hardly ever / eats / He
3. salad / lunch. / I / for / have / often
4. drink / doesn't / She / coffee. / often
5. July. / It / always / is / in / hot
6. sometimes / Saturdays. / We / shopping / go / on
7. home. / usually / They / at / breakfast / have

Yes or no?

Complete the answers. Put *Yes* or *No* in the spaces.

1. Q: Do they usually work on Saturdays?   A: ...., never.
2. Q: Do they drink water with their dinner?   A: ...., always.
3. Q: Does he buy magazines?   A: ...., sometimes.
4. Q: Does she go to work by car?   A: ...., usually.
5. Q: Does he usually walk to work?   A: ...., hardly ever.
6. Q: Do they eat in restaurants?   A: ...., not often.

Routines

Make sentences with these words.

every day   once a week   twice a week   three times a week

Name	Activity	Days of the week						
		M	T	W	T	F	S	S
Mike and Sarah	rent a DVD		✓					✓
David	read the newspaper	✓	✓	✓	✓	✓	✓	✓
Paul and Tania	go dancing						✓	
Anna	go to the gym	✓		✓		✓		

1 Mike and Sarah ....

2 David ....

3 Paul and Tania ....

4 Anna ....

Film questionnaire

Complete the questionnaire.

1 How often do you rent DVDs or videos?
   ☐ once or twice a month   ☐ two or three times a week
   ☐ hardly ever   ☐ never

2 Which of these things do you have at home?
   ☐ TV   ☐ DVD player
   ☐ video recorder   ☐ widescreen TV
   ☐ satellite/cable

3 How often do you watch films on television?
   ☐ every evening   ☐ often
   ☐ sometimes   ☐ never
   ☐ not often   ☐ hardly ever

4 How often do you go to the cinema?
   ☐ more than once a week ☐ once a week
   ☐ once a month   ☐ once a year   ☐ never

5 Do you usually watch the news on TV?
   ☐ always   ☐ usually   ☐ often
   ☐ sometimes   ☐ hardly ever   ☐ never

6 How many DVDs or videos do you buy a year?
   ☐ more than fifty   ☐ more than twelve   ☐ five or six
   ☐ one or two   ☐ none

7 Do you buy DVDs or videos as presents for people?
   ☐ sometimes   ☐ not often   ☐ never

twenty-two

Grammar: present simple or continuous?

1 **Read the text. Match the questions and answers.**
Jessica works in a bank. She usually gets up at 7.30 and goes to work. She didn't get up at 7.30 this morning because it's Sunday. She doesn't work on Sundays. It's 10.30 and she's still in bed. She's reading e-mails from her friends.

1 What does Jessica do?
2 When does she usually get up?
3 Did she get up at 7.30 this morning?
4 Why not?
5 What is she doing?

A Because it's Sunday.
B She's reading e-mails from her friends.
C She works in a bank.
D She gets up at 7.30.
E No, she didn't.

2 **Put these examples in the table.**
1 What is she doing?
2 What does she usually do?
3 What does she do?
4 She's reading e-mails.
5 She works in a bank.
6 She usually gets up at 7.30.

	questions	answers
Jobs, etc.		
Everyday routines		
Things happening now		

3 **Choose the correct words.**
Britanny and Gary (live / are living) in England, but they (don't / aren't) in England now. They both (work / are working) in a shop. They're on a beach in Spain. They (sunbathe / are sunbathing).

4 **Answer the questions about Brittany and Gary.**
1 Where do they live?
2 What does he do?
3 What does she do?
4 What do they do?
5 What is she doing?
6 What is he doing?
7 What are they doing?

Appearance

1 How many words can you add to the word map in two minutes?

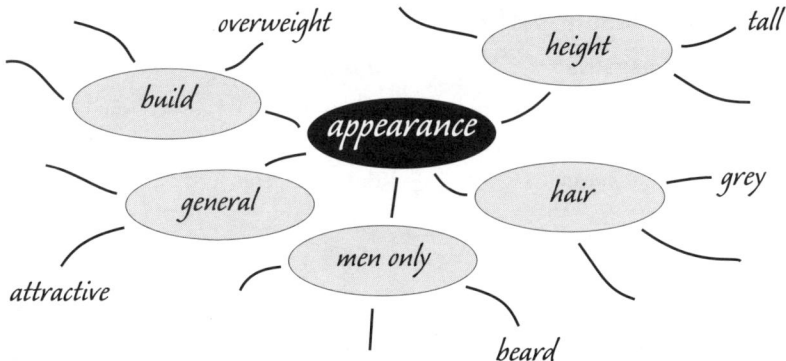

- appearance
  - build — overweight
  - height — tall
  - general — attractive
  - hair — grey
  - men only — beard

Responses

Match the questions and answers.

1. What colour are her eyes?
2. Has he got a moustache?
3. What size are you?
4. Does she wear glasses?
5. How old are the twins?
6. What's she wearing?
7. What's his hair like?

A A long blue dress.
B Extra large.
C They're twelve.
D It's brown and wavy.
E Yes, but only for driving.
F Yes, he has.
G They're brown.

How often? / When?

Look at these time expressions. Some of them tell us *when* something is happening, or happened. Some of them are frequency expressions. They tell us *how often* something happens or happened.

Underline the frequency expressions.

always	every day	yesterday	at six o'clock	sometimes
now	usually	every week	twice a month	last year
hardly ever	often	once a week	at the moment	never

Past tenses

Complete the table.

present	past
	ate
come	
	drank
forget	

present	past
	ran
take	
wear	

twenty-three

Grammar: present perfect

Positive and negative			Questions		
I, You, We, They	have 've haven't	been there. seen it.	Have	I, you, we, they	been there? seen it?
He, She, It	's has hasn't		Has	he, she, it	

Short answers	
Yes, (I) have.	No, (we) haven't.
Yes, (he) has.	No, (she) hasn't.

1 Look at the table. Complete the conversation.

A Hello, I .... seen you this week.

Have you .... on holiday?

B No, I .... been ill.

A Oh, dear. I'm sorry. .... you been to the doctor yet?

B Yes, I ....

A Did the doctor give you antibiotics?

B No, she didn't. It's just a virus. My husband's got it too.

A .... he been to the doctor?

B No, he ....

2 Complete the sentences with *ever*, *never*, or *yet*.

1 Has he been to the doctor ....?

2 Have you .... been to New York?

3 I've .... been to an opera.

4 He's .... seen a Shakespeare play.

5 Has she .... been to Ireland?

6 I haven't been shopping .... I'm going later.

How often have you been there?

Make sentences.

- I went to Scotland for the first time last year, and I went again this year.
  I've been to Scotland twice.
- I saw Madonna in concert for the first time last month.
  I've seen Madonna once.
1 We saw the *Mona Lisa* in Paris last week. It was our first time.
2 He went to Florida in 1999, 2001, and 2003.
3 They saw the film at 4.30 and loved it. So they saw it again at 8.15.

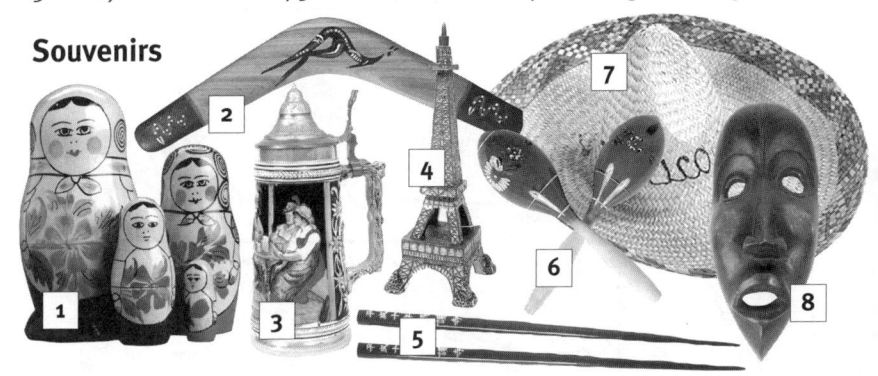

Souvenirs

Ann and Jeff are retired. They have been to eight different countries, and they always buy souvenirs. These are some souvenirs from their holidays.

1 **Identify the souvenirs. Put the numbers in the boxes.**
   ☐ some chopsticks   ☐ some dolls   ☐ a mask
   ☐ a boomerang   ☐ some maracas   ☐ a model Eiffel tower
   ☐ a sombrero   ☐ a beer mug

2 **Make sentences about the souvenirs.**

- *The dolls are Russian.*

3 **Make sentences about Ann and Jeff's holidays.**

- *They've been to Russia. They bought the dolls there.*

4 **Guess the answers to these questions. Write short answers.**

   Yes, they have.   No, they haven't.   I think so.   I don't think so.

1 Have they been to St. Petersburg? ....
2 Have they been to the top of the Eiffel Tower? ....
3 Have they seen wild elephants? ....
4 Have they seen the Berlin Wall? ....
5 Have they seen the Taj Mahal in India? ....

twenty-four

Seven ages

1. HAVEN'T YOU EATEN YOUR DINNER YET?
2. HAVEN'T YOU DONE YOUR HOMEWORK YET?
3. HASN'T HE FOUND A JOB YET?
4. HASN'T HE FINISHED HIS WORK YET?
5. HAVEN'T YOU FED THE BABY YET?
6. HAVEN'T YOU WASHED THE CAR YET?
7. HAVEN'T YOU EATEN YOUR DINNER YET?

Read the cartoon. Complete the table.

present	past	past participle
find	found	....
wash	washed	....
feed	fed	....
eat	ate	....
do	did	....
finish	finished	....

The next word

Put a cross (X) by any words that don't go with the words in bold.

- **Have you seen ...?** X UFO   X to look   ✓ *Titanic*   ✓ Martin Smith   ✓ it

Have you been ...? ☐ there ☐ to go ☐ anywhere ☐ to France
He has won ☐ $64,000 ☐ the competition ☐ never ☐ a prize
She has met ☐ we ☐ some famous people ☐ them ☐ David Beckham
Have you eaten ...? ☐ your dinner ☐ oysters ☐ enjoyed ☐ Chinese food
I've bought ☐ some postcards ☐ a DVD ☐ one ☐ to them
She's gone ☐ home ☐ to the bank ☐ here ☐ there

is / has / possessive 's

What does 's mean in these sentences? Write A *is*, B *has*, or C *possessive*.

1. She's ill. ☐
2. She's got a virus. ☐
3. Her husband's name is Jim. ☐
4. It's raining. ☐
5. He's gone to the pub. ☐
6. It's been very hot today. ☐
7. Paul's parents live in Dublin. ☐
8. She's seen the doctor twice. ☐

Word order

Put the words in the correct order to make sentences.

- yet? / Have / done / it / you   *Have you done it yet?*

1. been / She / bank. / just / the / to / 's
2. lunch. / gone / 've / to / They
3. often / We / France. / 've / to / been
4. competition. / never / I / won / 've / a
5. had / yet. / haven't / I / breakfast
6. elephant? / you / Have / an / seen / ever

CLOSED
Gone to lunch
If not back by five,
gone to dinner too.

Reminders

1 Read the text and the signs.

Most British car parks are 'pay and display'. You buy a ticket from a machine, and display the ticket in your car window.

HAVE YOU PAID AND DISPLAYED?
Car Parking Charges Applicable
7 Days per Week
Town Centre Shops →
← Beaches

WELCOME TO
BATH ROAD NORTH
PAY & DISPLAY
CAR PARK
P FIRST ENTRANCE ON THE LEFT P

Have you **Paid and Displayed** your ticket?

2 Find answers.
1. What's the past participle of *pay*?
2. Is *pay* a regular verb?
3. What's the past participle of *display*?
4. Is *display* a regular verb?
5. Which sentence is a 'reminder'?

twenty-five

Grammar: *will / won't*

Positive and negative			Questions			Short answers
I	'll	do it.	Will	I	do it?	Yes, (I) will.
You	will	be there.		you	be there?	No, (I) won't.
He	won't			he		
She	will not			she		
It				it		
We				we		
They				they		

Label the sentences with these words.

requesting   deciding   refusing   promising   offering   agreeing

Sentence   **Function**

1 It's seven o'clock. Hmm. I'll get up
   early and have a shower.   *deciding*

2 You look tired. I'll make you a cup of tea.   ....

3 I'm really sorry. It won't happen again.   ....

4 Will you help me with my homework?   ....

5 No! I won't do it! Don't ask again!   ....

6 Yes, you're right. I'll do it.   ....

Responses

Match.

1 I'll have a hamburger and fries.   A Yes, of course I will.
2 Give the doll to your sister now!   B I don't know. I'll tell you later.
3 Will you get me an aspirin?   C Yes, I'll have one too.
4 Phew! It's hot in here.   D Sorry, I'll do it tomorrow.
5 I'll have a beer. What about you?   E I'll open the window.
6 You haven't done your homework.   F OK. Anything else?
7 Would you like to go to a party
   on Saturday?   G No, mummy. I won't!

Word order

Put *never* or *ever* in these sentences.

- *I have **never** been to London.*
- *Will you **ever** learn to drive?*

1. I will get married.
2. Does he eat beef?
3. I am bored.
4. Will he walk again?
5. Has she studied English?
6. I will be rich.
7. She gets up before 10 a.m.

Conversations

Match the conversations to the people. Write the letter in the speech bubble.

A Bye. I'll see you later.
B OK. See you. Bye.

C Will you speak to Mark Kennedy?
D Not now. I'll phone him later.

E I'll open the bottle.
F OK, I'll cut the bread.

G Will you take this man to be your husband?
H I will.

I I won't tell you again! Don't speak to Jimmy.
J No, Miss. I won't.

K You'll feel OK tomorrow.
L Will I really?

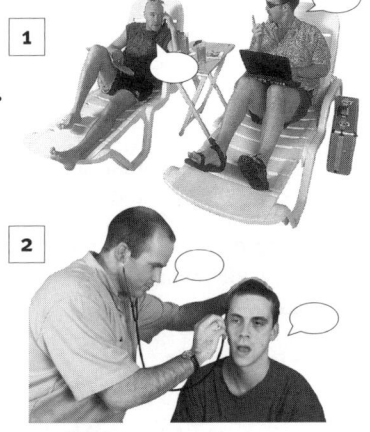

twenty-six

Grammar

past simple	present simple	future simple
was	am / is	will be
.....	are	.....
saw	see / sees	will see
.....	happen / happens	.....
.....	..... /	will go
did	..... /	.....

1 **Complete the table.**

2 **Complete the conversation.**

A Hi, it's Eric.
B Eric! Where are you? Have you landed already?
A Yeah, the flight was early. I'm at the airport. Can you pick me up now?
B Sure.

A How long .... you be?
B I'll .... there in fifteen minutes.

Where .... you be?
A .... be by the taxi stand.
B Leave your mobile on, and go and have a coffee or something. .... call you when I get to the airport.
A Great. Thanks. I'll .... you soon.

3 **Complete the sentences with these things.**

a number   a year   a birthday present   a month
a day of the week   a time

1 It'll be .... the day after tomorrow.
2 Next year will be ....
3 I'll get up at .... tomorrow.
4 I'll buy my teacher .... for his/her birthday.
5 I'll finish this unit in .... minutes.
6 I'll be on holiday next ....

E-mails

1 Match the replies to the e-mails.

e-mails

1 Jackie: Call me tomorrow. It's important. Phil
 * The contents of this e-mail are confidential. If you have received it in error, please forward to phil@admin.smith.inc.com

2 Michael: I tried to phone three times, but you weren't in. When can I speak to you? Sarah

3 Teresa: Thanks for the documents. I'll read them, and call you back on Tuesday morning. Tom

4 Dear Mrs Banner, Please confirm time of arrival on May 17. Yours Minnie Cook, Grand Hotel
 *** visit our website at www.grandhotels.com ***

5 Online Registration: You have registered your upgrade copy of MacroHard Sentence Version 15 serial number 043YTR789X320ZGT. You have not included your telephone number. Please send to this address. dennis.reg.23@MacroHard.uk.com

Replies

A Out-of-office auto reply: I will be away on Thursday and Friday. Please send any urgent messages to my secretary, Samantha. sam@westnet.co.uk

B Sorry, I won't be here on Tuesday. Can you phone on Wednesday? Any time after ten.

C I won't send my telephone number. I don't want any unsolicited phone calls.

D Good to hear from you. I'll call you after lunch.

E My plane arrives at 16.30. I'll get a taxi from the airport and I'll be there at about 18.00.

2 Write a short reply to this e-mail. It's from an old friend. You haven't seen him/her for several years.

> Hi!
> It's me! I got your e-mail address from a friend. I haven't seen you for years. What are you doing now? Do you still live at the same address? How's your family? Let me know. I'll be in your town next week. Send me your phone number, and I'll call you.
> Best wishes ...

twenty-seven

Grammar: comparison
Complete the table.

	adjective	comparative	superlative
short adjectives	long	longer	longest
short adjectives, ending with -e	large	larger	
	nice		nicest
adjectives ending in -y	friendly		friendliest
	dry	drier	
adjectives – double the last letter	big	bigger	
	hot		hottest
irregular	good		best
	bad	worse	
long adjectives	interesting	more interesting	
	expensive		most expensive

Comparatives

1 Complete.

Archie and Tessa are brother and sister. He's a year .... than her, and he's taller. She's shorter .... him, but she's got .... hair.

2 Rewrite these sentences. Put *better* in the correct places.
1 The weather is much than yesterday.
2 I'm a driver than my sister.
3 The price of petrol is here.
4 Sorry you were ill. Are you today?
5 She thinks she's than me, but she isn't!
6 Don't eat the chocolate. Have an apple. It's for you.

Superlatives

Match the beginning, middle, and end of these sentences.

Beginning	Middle	End
1 Sarah is	A the best singer	T by William Shakespeare.
2 The Grand Hotel is	B the worst one	U in her family.
3 The bass guitarist is	C the youngest	V of the year in Europe.
4 December 21st is	D the most popular team	W I've ever seen!
5 Manchester United is	E the shortest day	X in the city.
6 That horror film was	F the most famous play	Y in the group.
7 *Hamlet* is	G the most expensive	Z in England.

Signs

Read the signs.
1 List the comparatives.
2 List the superlatives.
3 In the signs, does *best* mean *cheapest* or *most expensive*?
4 You can advertise a pub as the *oldest*. Would you advertise a supermarket as the oldest?
5 *Bigger* describes the breakfast.
 Which of these words would you use to advertise breakfast?
 ☐ healthier ☐ smaller ☐ cheaper
 ☐ more expensive ☐ more fattening
6 The sign on the litter bin is positive.
 If you put your litter in the bin, the town will be better, cleaner, etc.
 Write a negative sign.
 Begin: *If you don't put your litter in this bin, the town will be ...*

twenty-eight

Grammar: adverbs of manner

1 Complete the table with adverbs of manner.

	adjective	adverb
regular + -ly	slow	slowly
	quick	....
	bad	....
ending in -y ➡ -ily	noisy	noisily
	easy	....
	angry	....
no change	fast	fast
	hard	hard
irregular	good	well

2 Underline the adverbs of manner and circle the frequency adverbs.
1 He doesn't usually work on Fridays.
2 She spoke quietly and slowly.
3 He did the job very well.
4 It always rains at weekends!
5 They phoned the police immediately.

3 Complete the sentences with these words.

> too   again   another   both   other   already

1 You've done one exercise. Do .... one.
2 Ted and Jane were .... late for the class.
3 He's got red hair and she's got red hair ....
4 'Be quiet! I won't tell you ....'
5 This song is good. It's better than the .... ones.
6 I was early for the class, but the teacher was .... there.

The next word

Put a cross (✗) by any words that don't go with the verbs.

- **drive**   ✓ carefully   ✗ bad   ✓ well   ✓ slowly

fall   ☐ badly   ☐ down   ☐ into something   ☐ good
read   ☐ difficult   ☐ the book   ☐ carefully   ☐ fast
run   ☐ fast   ☐ quickly   ☐ beautiful   ☐ to school
speak   ☐ quietly   ☐ loudly   ☐ angrily   ☐ him

Reading

Match the extracts to the book titles.
A *Barry Foster and the Magic Key* – K.J. Towelling
B *The Big Book of Pop Stars* – Mark Greeley
C *Puzzles with Maths* – Sharon Einstein
D *Love in the Office* – Barbara Carter
E *By Train Through Siberia* – Oliver O. Hornby
F *Goal! The Gary Smith Story* – Gary Smith

1 The funniest TV interview with Eye Dolls was with Shaun Clancy. The interviewer said, 'Do you write all your own songs?' 'Oh, yes,' said Shaun. 'So did you write "Please Love Me"?' 'Yes, I did, it was our biggest hit,' said Shaun. The interviewer smiled, 'So, what key is it in?' Of course Shaun didn't know. ☐

2 People often ask me, 'So what is the key to your very successful career?' It's a difficult question. But I have been the best player in every team I've ever played in. I've scored more goals, run faster, and been the most popular with the fans. And I've never been big-headed. ☐

3 The old man had long white hair, and strange yellow eyes.
  'So this is the terrible Brago Fumidor,' thought Barry.
The old man laughed, and his sharp teeth were even yellower than his eyes, 'Well, young man,' he hissed, 'You've come here for the gold key to the thirteenth door.' ☐

4 Rosalind's beautiful, long fingers tapped at the keyboard softly. Gareth sat at his desk, only two metres away, but he didn't look in her direction. She thought about their last argument, about their last kiss. A tear fell quietly. She looked down. The tear was there ... exactly on the key for G. G for Gareth. ☐

5 Is maths boring? Not if you try these fantastic games and puzzles! There are five hundred puzzles in this book. Always do the puzzles first, then you can look at the answer key on pages 267 to 298. ☐

6 On the fifth day, I looked out of the window. Trees, trees, and more trees. An old woman gave me her map to look at. The key had symbols for mountains, lakes, rivers and cities. She pointed her finger at the map, 'We are here,' she said carefully. She spoke English well, but slowly. The only symbols on that part of the map were trees. And more trees. ☐

Dictionary skills

Read the definition of *key*. Find the six meanings in the book extracts and write the numbers of the definitions in the boxes.

☆ **key¹** /kiː/ *noun* [C] **1** a metal object that is used for locking or unlocking a door, etc.: *Have you seen my car keys anywhere?* ○ *We need a spare key to the front door.* ○ *a bunch of keys* **2** a set of musical notes that is based on one particular note: *The piece is in the key of A minor.* **3** one of the parts of a piano, typewriter, etc. that you press with your fingers to make it work **4** a set of answers to exercises or problems: *The key to the crossword will appear in next week's issue.* **5** a list of the symbols and signs used in a map or book, showing what they mean **6** [usually sing.] something that helps you achieve or understand sth: *A good education is the key to success.* ○ *This letter holds the key to the mystery.*

twenty-nine

Grammar: *have to* for obligation

present simple	I, You, We, They	have / 've got	to	do it.
	He, She, It	has / 's got		be there.
past simple	I, You, We, They, He, She, It	had		
present perfect	I, You, We, They	have / 've had		
	He, She, It	has / 's had		
future	I, You, We, They, He, She, It	will have		

Questions					
present simple	Do	I, you, we, they	have	to	do it?
	Does	he, she, it			be there?
past simple	Did	I, you, we, they, he, she, it	have		
present perfect	Have	I, you, we, they	had		
	Has	he, she, it			
future	Will	I, you, we, they, he, she, it	have		

1 Look at the table. Complete the short answers.

Questions	Positive short answers	Negative short answers
Do you have to get up early?	Yes, …………	No, …………
Does she have to help her parents?	Yes, …………	No, …………
Did we have to work hard?	Yes, …………	No, …………
Have you had to use a dictionary?	Yes, …………	No, …………
Has he had to get a passport?	Yes, …………	No, …………
Will they have to do an exam?	Yes, …………	No, …………

2 Tick (✓) the correct words.
1 She couldn't (☐ speak ☐ to speak ☐ speaking) English.
2 (☐ Did he can ☐ Was he can ☐ Could he) get a job?
3 We (☐ didn't can ☐ weren't can ☐ couldn't) go to the party.
4 Could he understand the last lesson?
   No, he (☐ didn't ☐ can't ☐ couldn't).
5 Why (☐ don't ☐ couldn't ☐ haven't) you go to the party last night?

3 Complete the sentences with *could* or *couldn't*.

Positive	I .... speak English last year.
Negative	He .... drive last year.
Questions	.... you swim when you were ten?
Short answers	Yes, I .... No, I ....

Changing places

1 Read the introduction, then complete the text with *had to* and *couldn't*.

> Samantha Spencer is a business executive, and she works for a group of hotels. For a TV programme, she changed places with a cleaner in one of the hotels. Her life changed completely. The cameras filmed her new life for a month.

> She had to live on the cleaner's wages. These were 80% less than her salary as an executive. She .... live in a cheap flat in the city centre. She .... drive her car, because petrol was too expensive. She .... work from 6 a.m to 3 p.m. every day, and she .... wear a uniform. After a week, she .... get a second job because she didn't have enough money for food. Her flat was 75% of her wages. She worked in the evenings in a supermarket. She didn't have any free time, so she .... meet her friends. She .... save any money because she .... spend all her wages on rent, food, and bus travel. She got very depressed and she was very happy when the month was over. 'I .... do that again,' she said.

2 Answer the questions.
1. Where did she have to live?
2. What did she have to wear?
3. Why couldn't she drive her car?
4. What hours did she have to work?
5. Why did she have to get a second job?
6. Why couldn't she meet her friends?
7. Why couldn't she save any money?

Responses

Match the questions and answers.

1. Could you swim when you were ten?
2. Were you at the party last night?
3. Do you have to work on Sundays?
4. Do you wear a uniform at work?
5. Are you coming to the beach on Saturday?

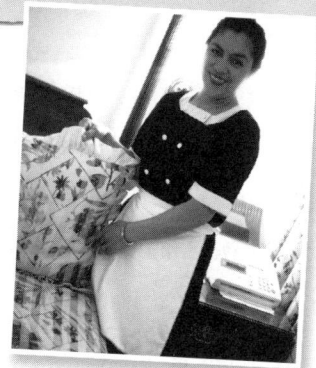

A   Sometimes, but not usually.
B   Sorry. I've got to work.
C   No, I couldn't go. I had to work.
D   Yes, but not very far.
E   No, but I have to wear a suit.

thirty

Grammar

I, You, We, They	want don't want 'd like wouldn't like	to	be rich. go to New York. lose weight.
He, She	wants doesn't want 'd like wouldn't like		

Choose the correct form of the verb (infinitive / bare infinitive / -ing form) and complete the sentences. Use the verb in brackets.

infinitive: *to do*   bare infinitive: *do*   -ing form: *doing*

1 I want .... famous. (be)
2 I'd like .... to another country. (move)
3 I like .... football. (watch)
4 I'm .... to the doctor tomorrow. (go)
5 I can't .... Italian. (speak)
6 I've got .... early tomorrow. (get up)
7 I didn't have .... a uniform at school. (wear)
8 I'm going .... a holiday next month. (have)
9 I could .... the piano when I was six. (play)

Futures

Add one word to each of the sentences.

- *Where would you like **to** go?*
1 Would you to go to the cinema tomorrow?
2 I'll there at 10.30.
3 I want be rich one day.
4 It's to rain tomorrow.
5 He like to travel to the Moon.

Connecting

Connect the beginnings and endings of the sentences with one of these words.

> and   so   but   because

1 He wants to be a doctor .... he hasn't got any qualifications.
2 I'd like to go to Rome .... Venice too.
3 They got married in 2001 .... they got divorced in 2002.
4 She had to take antibiotics .... she was ill.
5 He wanted to go to China .... he had to get a visa.
6 I couldn't program the video .... I couldn't understand the instructions.
7 I missed the bus .... I was late for work.

Choose a conversation

All the responses are correct English. Choose and make a conversation.

1 A Let's go out this evening.
  B - Where do you want to go?
     - OK, let's go out.
     - Great idea.
2 A How about going to the cinema?
  B - What do you want to see?   - All right. What's on?
     - Yes, I'd like to see a film.
3 A *Kiss of the Dragon* is at the UGC multiplex.
  B - I hate kung-fu films.   - No, I've seen it twice.
     - I don't want to see that.
4 A What would you like to see?
  B - How about *Harry Potter*?
     - I'd like to see *Harry Potter*.
     - Let's see *Harry Potter*.
5 A I don't want to see that.
  B - Why not?
     - Why don't you like it?
     - What's the reason?
6 A Because it's a kids' film.
  B - I like watching kids' films.
     - It's had good reviews.
     - I liked the last one.
7 A Oh, do we have to?
  B - Yes, you'll enjoy it.
     - Not if you don't want to.
     - We can see something else.

Answer key

ANSWER KEY

Note: *e.g.* (for example) means that there is more than one possible correct answer. *Free* means **you** choose the answers.

one

Grammar: *be* singular
You're / He's / He isn't / She isn't / Are you …? / Is she …?

Personal information
Title / Family name / First name / Nationality / Telephone number

Responses
1D   2E   3B   4F   5C   6A

Numbers
A three   B eight   C nine   D seven
E five   F four   G six   H one   I zero

Writing: capital letters
1 Patrick's from Dublin in Ireland.
2 Nice to meet you, Josh.
3 London's in England.
4 Pepsi is American.

Reading: countries and nationalities
1 Japanese, American
2 American, the USA
3 Austrian, Hungarian
4 Russia, English
5 Italian, British
6 French, Egypt, Egyptian

two

Grammar: *be* plural
We're / They're / We aren't / They aren't / Are we …? / Are they …?
Possessive adjectives: your / his / her / our / their

Short answers: *be*
1 No, she isn't.   5 Yes, he is.
2 Yes, we are.   6 No, they aren't.
3 No, I'm not.   7 Yes, she is.
4 Yes, I am.   8 Yes, they are.

Possessive adjectives
1 Your   2 His   3 Their   4 Our   5 Her

Numbers: date of birth
1 three / twelve / seventy-seven
2 twenty-one / eight / oh one
3 thirty / seven / eighty-seven
4 sixteen / one / oh three
5 fifteen / five / fifty-five
6 twenty-two / two / ninety-nine
7 eleven / three / ninety-four
8 thirteen / four / sixty-eight
9 fourteen / ten / forty-nine

Greetings
'Hello' only: Hi!, Hey!
'Goodbye' only: See you tonight., Bye., Goodnight., See you.
'Hello' or 'Goodbye': Good morning., Good afternoon., Good evening.

Responses
1D   2C   3F   4E   5G   6B   7A

three

Grammar: *a / an*
1 1 an   2 a   3 a   4 a   5 an   6 an
   7 an   8 a   9 a   10 an   11 an   12 a
2 They are all true.

Writing: question marks and full stops
1 ? / .   2 ? / .   3 ? / .   4 ? / . / ?   5 . / ? / ?

and, or
1 or   2 and   3 or   4 and   5 and   6 or

Word + word
1 Morning coffee + Morning coffees / Afternoon teas / Evening meals
2 express lunch / light lunches / business lunches
3 hot & cold, coffees & teas, wines & spirits, fish & chips
4 breakfasts, lunches, lunch, dinner, evening meals
5 free (sandwich, baguette, restaurant, brasserie, express, pizza)

four

Grammar: demonstrative pronouns
1 singular: this (near), that (far)
  plural: these (near), those (far)
2 lunches, paintings, guides, seats, entrances, glasses, potatoes

Responses
1E   2G   3A   4D   5F   6B   7C

Colours
1 Black   2 Pink   3 grey   4 Red
5 orange   6 purple   7 white
8 Brown   9 yellow   10 green

Numbers
1 Two hundred and seventy-six
2 Forty-three thousand
3 Fifty-seven
4 Three thousand four hundred and five
5 Sixty-two thousand nine hundred and sixty-one
6 One thousand five hundred

Quiz
1 What colour, yellow
2 Who, William Shakespeare
3 Where, in Canada
4 How old, four thousand
5 Where, England
6 What, Canberra
7 What, Motor-car racing
8 What, American

five

Grammar: *have got / has got*
1 You / We / They have got, You / We / They've got, You / We / They have not got, You / We / They haven't got, Have you / we / they got …?
She / It has got, She / It's got, She / It has not got, She / It hasn't got, Has she / it got …?
2 ('I …' is a free answer)
Picture 3: David hasn't got a dictionary. Anna hasn't got a dictionary. (OR They haven't got dictionaries.)
Picture 4: David hasn't got any boots. Anna hasn't got any boots. (OR They haven't got any boots.)
Picture 5: David's got some gloves. Anna's got some gloves (OR They've got some gloves.)
Picture 6: David hasn't got a personal stereo. Anna's got a personal stereo.

Family words
male: father / uncle / son / brother / nephew
female: wife / granddaughter

Responses
1 D 2 F 3 A 4 G 5 C 6 B 7 E

Writing: apostrophes
1 ha 2 ha 3 o 4 a 5 o 6 o 7 i
8 a 9 i

six

Grammar: present simple
1 sell / works / don't know / doesn't work / Do you know? / Does she work? / Yes, I do.
2 1 does, works, 2 Does, does, 3 does, sells, 4 Does, doesn't, 5 does, works

Reading
(e.g.) 1 A 2 B, C 3 A 4 B, C 5 C
6 A, B, C 7 A 8 B, C 9 B, C 10 A
11 B, C 12 A 13 A, B 14 B 15 A
16 C 17 B 18 C (B?) 19 A 20 C

The next word
✗ (= wrong) words: retired / us / work in a shop / salesperson / at university

seven

Grammar
1 Is / Are
an / a / some / any
2 1 There 2 any 3 many 4 It
5 are 6 It is 7 a

Articles: *a / an, the,* 'zero' article
– / – / the / the / an / a / a / a / an

Using your dictionary: plurals
beaches, art galleries, universities, boys, cities, theatres, addresses

Writing: capital letters
1 Free
2 Liverpool is a city in the county of Lancashire in England. The city is on the River Mersey and was famous in the 1960s for the music of The Beatles. There are two famous football teams in the city, Liverpool and Everton. The old docks are now a tourist attraction. There are two art galleries, the Walker Art Gallery and the Tate Gallery. Liverpool has two cathedrals. The airport is seven miles from the city, and it is called John Lennon Airport after the Beatle, who was murdered in 1980.

ANSWER KEY

eight

Time
Analogue: twelve o'clock / five past eleven / twenty past seven / half past nine / twenty-five to seven / quarter to eleven / five to nine
Digital: eight ten / four fifteen / two twenty-five / twelve forty / four fifty

Arrivals and departures
A2   B3   C5   D1   E6   F4

Find the information
1 16.50   2 20.20   3 11.10
4 11 hours   5 No.

get
Free

nine

Grammar: pronouns
me / you / him / her / it / us / them

Reading: signs
1 Look right and left = Look both ways
2 Be careful = Watch out
3 area = zone
4 24 hours = Day and night

Imperatives
1   1 Come in   2 help me   3 Turn on
    4 Watch out   5 turn off   6 Don't forget
2   Free

Prepositions
1   1 A8   2 E2   3 B14   4 D7   5 H4
    6 C8   7 B6
2   (e.g.) E15 is at the end of the row at the back.
    F5 is in the balcony (at the front).
    J1 is on the left at the back in the balcony.
    E8 is in the middle of the row at the back.
    D5 is on the left (near the back)
    A14 is on the right (in the front).
    G10 is in the balcony (on the right).

ten

Grammar: *can / can't*
1   1 speak   2 Can he   3 can't   4 can't
    5 Can
2   can / can't / Can / can / can't

Word map
Free

Mobile phone
1   (e.g.) can't / train / at / me / not / a / take / to / 's / Can / you
2   (e.g.) When does it arrive? / Sorry, I can't. / I'm busy. / 40 minutes. / Yes, you can. / Bye. / Bye. / Bye.

Abilities
1 True.   2 True.
3 False. They can swim well.
4 False. The record is 81 years. The average is 60 years.
5 True. One type can swim at 55 k/h. Most types can swim at 40 k/h.
6 False.
7 True.
8 True. The record is 36 years. The average is 13–15 years.
9 True, but only when humans teach them.
10 False. The record is 1 metre 75 centimetres.
11 False. They can swim and fly.
12 True.

Writing: contractions
1 I am not   2 She is not   3 We are not
4 I have got   5 He has got   6 I do not
7 It does not   8 I cannot

eleven

Grammar: countable and uncountable
1   people / chips / messages / milk / rice / petrol
2   1 yogurt (U), 2 beans (C), 3 food (U),
    4 meat (U), 5 salad (U), 6 eggs (C),
    7 water (U), 8 nuts (C), 9 bread (U),
    10 sugar (U), 11 grapes (C),
    12 vegetables (C), 13 flour (U),
    14 chocolate (U), 15 chocolates (C),
    16 slices of bread (C), 17 butter (U),
    18 litres of water (C), 19 soup (U),
    20 cans of beer (C)

3 Countable: coins, Canadian dollars, notes, bills, Australian dollars, magazines, onions, onion rings
Uncountable: money, Canadian money, paper, coal, onion

Possessive 's
1 There's some water in the glass. (is)
2 Is that Sarah's car? (poss)
3 St James's Palace is in London. (poss)
4 Michael's got some salad on his plate. (has)
5 Whose cup's this? (is)
6 Do you know Paul's sister? (poss)
7 Anna's got a new boyfriend. (has)
8 Where's Sandra? (is)

Quiz
1 How old, about 500 years
2 What, oil
3 Which, Liverpool
4 Where, Seattle, USA
5 Who, Queen Elizabeth
6 When, 14th February

twelve

Grammar: *would like*
1 1 How many tickets would you like?
  2 I'd like another one please.
  3 How much ice would you like?
  4 I'd like some of these please.
  5 Which one would she like?
2 'd / Would / would / wouldn't

Responses
1F 2D 3A 4B 5C 6E

Countable / uncountable
1 biscuits 2 many 3 much 4 time
5 water 6 is 7 are 8 does 9 do 10 a

How many?
1 Example sentence (50)
  1 How many letters are there in the English alphabet? (26)
  2 How many players are there in a baseball team? (9)
  3 How many kilometres are there in a mile? (1.6)
  4 How many degrees are there in a circle? (360)

How much?
2 Example sentence (80%)
  1 How much of the Earth's surface is water? (71%)
  2 How much of the land on the Earth is desert? (12%)
  3 How much of the land on the Earth is under ice? (10%)
  4 How much of the human body is water? (70%)

thirteen

Symbols
1 1 coffee shop 2 restaurant 3 toilets
  4 bar 5 telephone 6 lift 7 escalator
  8 car park 9 information 10 cashpoint

Responses
1D 2G 3A 4B 5C 6E 7F

Asking for help
trying / along / end / third / the / miss / There's / far / not / in

Directions
1 A: left, along, second, left
  B: past, next, upstairs
2 Free

fourteen

Grammar: present continuous
'm / 're / 's / isn't
Are / Is
you / we / the / he
No, they aren't.

Responses
1C 2D 3F 4A 5B 6E

Christmas Day
1 Clockwise from top left: Jodie, Paul, Dylan, Jessica, Fiona, Jake
2 1 are they, eating 2 sitting, They're, on
  3 taking, Jessica 4 holding, is 5 's, He's
  6 pouring, is 7 's, talking, She's, to

fifteen

Grammar: likes and dislikes
1 Positive / Negative: watching TV. / tennis. / coffee. / dancing.
  Questions: watching TV? / tennis? / coffee? / dancing?
  Requests: some beer? / coffee?
2 Do / play / I don't / going / watching / I / I play / I play
3 loves / doesn't / likes / going / watching / loves / plays

like, would like, love
(e.g.) I love your tie! / Would you like tea or coffee? / What do you like doing in your free time? / I'd like a cheeseburger, please. / Do you like classical music? / Does he love me? / Does she love me?

The next word
✗ (= wrong) words: playing chess / anything else / driving / speak in class / work

sixteen

Grammar
Arrangements: 2, 4
Talking about the future: 3, 6
Future intentions: 1, 7
Suggestions: 5, 8

The next word
✗ (= wrong) words: going to the cinema / go home / studying / arrives / snowing

Question words
1 Where 2 What time 3 How long
4 What 5 How much 6 How many
7 Which

Reading
Free

seventeen

Grammar: past simple *be*
1 wasn't / weren't
was / wasn't / were / weren't
2 1 We weren't at home last night.
2 She was born in Canada.
3 He wasn't in his office yesterday.
4 Where were you last Saturday evening? 5 She was asleep at ten o'clock last night.
6 The children were very noisy.

Dates
(a) 1st December 2005 / 2nd October 1996 / 3rd September 2004 / 4th June 2000 / 5th August 1999 / 11th July 2006
(b) January 12th 2005 / February 10th 1996 / March 9th 2004 / April 6th 2000 / May 8th 1999 / November 7th 2006

Twentieth-century faces
1 1 were 2 were, was, wasn't 3 was, wasn't, was, was 4 was 5 was, was

2 1 Jacqueline Kennedy, Eva Perón
2 the Queen Mother 3 Tolkien
4 the Queen Mother 5 Laika
6 Tolkien 7 Bruce Lee, Eva Perón
8 the Queen Mother 9 Bruce Lee
10 the Queen Mother, Tolkien
11 Eva Perón 12 John F. Kennedy, Eva Perón 13 Jacqueline Kennedy, Eva Perón 14 the Queen Mother
3 Free

eighteen

Grammar: past simple – irregular verbs
1 had
go / didn't
Did / have
didn't
2 wasn't / weren't / did
had / bought / got / flew
went / saw
3 1B 2D 3E 4C 5A

The next word
✗ (= wrong) words: be cold / got / he / departure / happy

Shopping lists
1 free
2 1 bananas, red grapes, tomatoes*
2 salad, mixed vegetables, new potatoes, tomatoes* (*In conversation we think of tomatoes as a vegetable. A biologist will say that technically they are fruit.)
3 coffee (HP Sauce = brown sauce)
4 Parmesan cheese, tomato ketchup
3 1 Italy 2 Jamaica 3 red 4 strawberry

Writing
Free

nineteen

Grammar and spelling: regular verbs
+ *-ed*: wanted, started
+ *-d*: died, divorced, moved, phoned, liked, hated, lived
-y + *-ed*: played, stayed
-y, → *-ied*: married, studied, replied
double letter + *-ed*: travelled, stopped

Reading: a biography
1 became, danced, went, retired, sold, created, directed, moved, saw, starred, won, toured, started

2 1 16 July 1958   2 Riverdance, Lord of the Dance, Feet of Flames
3 Chicago, New York, Dallas   4 Dublin
5 California, Texas   6 The Chieftains

3 e.g. 1 He went to Ireland.   2 He started dancing.   3 He won the All-World Irish Dancing Championship.   4 He created Riverdance / He became a star.
5 He retired. / He did his final show.

Connecting: and / but
1 but   2 and   3 and   4 but   5 but   6 and

Writing: autobiography
Free

twenty

Grammar: subject and object questions
1 Who phoned Jacqui? / Who did John phone?
2 Who forgot her book? / What did Anna forget?
3 Who brought the wine? / What did Sarah bring?
4 Who kissed Tony? / Who did Angela kiss?
5 Who interviewed Shaun? / Who did Zoe interview?
6 Who carried the shopping? / What did Chris carry?

Past tenses
brought, came, fell, gave, held, carried, drew, forgot, paid, put, ran, took, thought, wrote

History
1 and 2   1F (painted)   2I (died)
3B (went)   4J (ended)   5A (fell)
6C (lived)   7D (wrote)   8E (started)
9G (created)   10H (flew)

3 1 Who   2 How   3 Where   4 When
5 What   6 Where   7 Who   8 Which
9 Who   10 What

4 1 What did Leonardo da Vinci paint?
7 What did Vivaldi write?
9 What did Matt Groening create?

twenty-one

Grammar: frequency adverbs
1 always / usually / often / sometimes / not often / hardly ever / never
2 1 They are never late.
2 He hardly ever eats fish.
3 I often have salad for lunch.
4 She doesn't often drink coffee.
5 It is always hot in July.
6 We sometimes go shopping on Saturdays.
7 They usually have breakfast at home.

Yes or No?
1 No   2 Yes   3 Yes   4 Yes   5 No   6 No
never, hardly ever, not often are negative.

Routines
1 Mike and Sarah rent a DVD twice a week.
2 David reads the newspaper every day.
3 Paul and Tania go dancing once a week.
4 Anna goes to the gym three times a week.

Film questionnaire
Free

twenty-two

Grammar: present simple or continuous?
1 1C   2D   3E   4A   5B
2 Jobs, etc: What does she do? / She works in a bank.
Everyday routines: What does she usually do? / She usually gets up at 7.30.
Things happening now: What is she doing? / She's reading e-mails.
3 live / aren't / work / are sunbathing
4 1 They live in England.   2 He works in a shop.   3 She works in a shop.
4 They work in a shop.   5 She's sunbathing.   6 He's sunbathing.
7 They're sunbathing.

Appearance
Free

Responses
1G   2F   3B   4E   5C   6A   7D

How often? / When?
always / every day / sometimes / usually / every week / twice a month / hardly ever / often / once a week / never

Past tenses
eat	ate
come	came
drink	drank
forget	forgot
run	ran
take	took
wear	wore

ANSWER KEY

twenty-three

Grammar: present perfect
1 haven't / been / 've / Have / have / Has / he hasn't
2 1 yet 2 ever 3 never 4 never 5 ever 6 yet

How often have you been there?
1 We've seen the Mona Lisa once.
2 We've been to Florida three times.
3 They've seen the film twice.

Souvenirs
1 some chopsticks 5 / a boomerang 2 / a sombrero 7 / some dolls 1 / some maracas 6 / a beer mug 3 / a mask 8 / a model Eiffel tower 4
2 2 The boomerang is Australian.
3 The beer mug is German.
4 The model Eiffel tower is French.
5 The chopsticks are Japanese.
6 The maracas are Spanish.
7 The sombrero is Mexican.
8 The mask is African.
3 Free
4 Free

twenty-four

Seven ages
found, washed. fed, eaten, done, finished

The next word
✗ (= wrong) words: to go / never / we / enjoyed / to them / here

is, has, possessive 's
1A 2B 3C 4A 5B 6B 7C 8B

Word order
1 She's just been to the bank.
2 They've gone to lunch.
3 We've often been to France.
4 I've never won a competition.
5 I haven't had breakfast yet.
6 Have you ever seen an elephant?

Reminders
2 1 paid 2 no 3 displayed 4 yes
5 Have you paid and displayed?

twenty-five

Grammar: will / won't
1 deciding 2 offering 3 promising
4 requesting 5 refusing 6 agreeing

Responses
1F 2G 3A 4E 5C 6D 7B

Word order
1 I will never get married.
2 Does he ever eat beef?
3 I am never bored.
4 Will he ever walk again?
5 Has she ever studied English?
6 I will never be rich.
7 She never gets up before 10 a.m.

Conversations
1C / D 2K / L 3I / J 4E / F
5A / B 6G / H

twenty-six

Grammar
1 were / happened / went
go / goes do / does
will be / will happen / will do
2 will / be / will / I'll / I'll / see
3 Free, but the answers will be …
1 a day of the week 2 a year
3 a time 4 a birthday present
5 a number 6 a month

e-mails
1 1D 2A 3B 4E 5C
2 Free

twenty-seven

Grammar: comparison
1 comparative: nicer / friendlier / hotter / better / more expensive
superlative: largest / driest / biggest / worst / most interesting

Comparatives
1 older / than / longer
2 1 The weather is much better than yesterday.
2 I'm a better driver than my sister.
3 The price of petrol is better here.
4 Sorry you were ill. Are you better today?
5 She thinks she's better than me, but she isn't!

6 Don't eat the chocolate. Have an apple. It's better for you.

Superlatives
(e.g.) CU 2GX 3AY 4EV 5DZ 6BW 7FT

Signs
1 better, greener, safer, cleaner, bigger, better
2 oldest, best, best
3 cheapest
4 No!
5 (e.g.) healthier, (possibly) cheaper
6 worse, dirtier, more dangerous, (uglier, unhealthier, ...)

twenty-eight

Grammar: adverbs of manner
quickly / badly
easily / angrily
2 1 He doesn't (usually) work on Fridays.
   2 She spoke quietly and slowly.
   3 He did the job very well.
   4 It (always) rains at weekends!
   5 They phoned the police immediately.
3 1 another 2 both 3 too 4 again 5 other 6 already

The next word
✗ (= wrong) words: good / difficult / beautiful / him

Reading
A3 B1 C D E F2

Dictionary skills
1 Definition 2   4 Definition 3
2 Definition 6   5 Definition 4
3 Definition 1   6 Definition 5

twenty-nine

Grammar: *have to* for obligation
1 positive: I do / she does / we did / I have / he has / they will.
  negative: I don't / she doesn't / we didn't / I haven't / he hasn't / they won't
2 1 speak 2 Could he 3 couldn't
   4 couldn't 5 couldn't
3 could / couldn't / Could / could / couldn't

Changing places
1 had to / couldn't / had to / had to / had to / couldn't / couldn't / had to / couldn't
2 (e.g.) 1 She had to live in a cheap flat.
  2 She had to wear a uniform.
  3 Because petrol was too expensive.
  4 She had to work from 6 a.m. to 3 p.m.
  5 Because she didn't have enough money for food. / She couldn't live on her wages.
  6 Because she didn't have any free time.
  7 Because she had to spend all her wages on rent, food and bus travel.

Responses
1D 2C 3A 4E 5B

thirty

Grammar
1 to be   2 to move   3 watching
4 going   5 speak   6 to get up
7 to wear   8 to have   9 play

Futures
1 Would you like to go to the cinema tomorrow?
2 I'll be there at 10.30.
3 I want to be rich one day.
4 It's going to rain tomorrow.
5 He'd like to travel to the Moon. (or He would ...)

Connecting
1 but   2 and   3 and / but   4 because
5 so   6 because   7 so

Choose a conversation
Free

Audio exercises

Introduction

You can do the audio exercises many times. Come back and repeat them in a week, and then in a month (and in a year). Try to do them faster. Try to do them without reading. Try to follow the stress, intonation, and word-linking patterns.

You can do these things:
- Listen to the exercises.
- Listen and read the exercises.
- Listen, read, and do the audio exercises.
- Close the book. Listen to the exercises.
- Close the book. Listen and do the audio exercises.

The audio exercises help you with many things. Here are some examples.

Grammar habits
They help you with habits – *He + does, they + do, we + have, she + has*. These things will become automatic if you practise. You won't need to think about them.
Track 16: *have* or *has*?
Track 34: *Is there any (meat)? / Are there any (potatoes)?*
Track 89: Responses with *Yes, I have. / Yes, she does. / Yes, she can.*, etc.

Word order
Track 67: *I usually get up early.*

Formulas
Track 97: *Sorry. I've got to go.*

Pronunciation
The sound of words.
Track 22: the /ðə/ the /ðiː/
Track 61: /t/ /d/ /ɪd/ endings for the past simple

Weak forms / Unstressed forms
Track 33: weak form of *can*
Track 54: *was* /wəz/ and *were* /wə/

Intonation
The way the voice goes up or down.
Track 11: *Anything to eat?*

Stress / Emphasis
Track 39: *Would you like this one or that one?*

Word linking
Track 10: *bread 'n' butter*
Track 19: *What do you do? (What d'you do?)*

If you want more practice with audio exercises like this, try the 3-in-1 Practice Pack for the Starter level of *In English*. They are easier.

Unit one

(*1) Copyright information

(*2) Reply.

- Good to meet you.
- ▶ *Good to meet you too.*
- Good to meet you too.

- Good to meet you.
- Pleased to meet you.
- Nice to meet you.
- Great to meet you.

(*3) Make questions.

- he
- ▶ *Where's he from?*
- Where's he from?

- you
- ▶ *Where are you from?*
- Where are you from?

- she
- you
- he

(*4) Repeat the numbers.

9 8 7 6 5 4 3 2 1
0 2 4 6 8
1 3 5 7 9

(*5) Reply.

- Bye. See you tomorrow.
- ▶ *Yes, see you tomorrow.*
- Yes, see you tomorrow.

- Goodbye. See you next lesson.
- Bye. See you later.
- Bye. See you again.

Unit two

(*6) Reply.

- Good morning.
- ▶ *Good morning.*
- Good morning.

- Good afternoon.
- Good evening.
- Goodnight.
- Goodbye.

(*7) Make questions.

- they
- ▶ *How old are they?*
- How old are they?

- she
- ▶ *How old is she?*
- How old is she?

- he
- you
- she
- they

(*8) Make sentences.

- we – our
- ▶ *We're in our classroom.*
- We're in our classroom.

- she – her
- ▶ *She's in her classroom.*
- She's in her classroom.

- they – their
- I – my
- he – his
- we – our
- you – your
- she – her

Unit three

(✱ 9) *a* or *an*?

- cup of tea
- ▶ *A cup of tea, please.*
- A cup of tea, please.

- egg sandwich
- ▶ *An egg sandwich, please.*
- An egg sandwich, please.

- espresso
- tuna sandwich
- mineral water
- apple juice

(✱ 10) *and* ('*n*')

- bread, butter
- ▶ *bread 'n' butter*
- bread 'n' butter

- egg, bacon
- salt, pepper
- milk, sugar
- rock, roll

(✱ 11) Reply with *no*.

- Anything to eat?
- ▶ *No, thanks.*
- No, thanks.

- Anything to drink?
- Anything else?
- Anything to eat?

(✱ 12) Reply.

- Thanks.
- ▶ *You're welcome.*
- You're welcome.

- Thank you.
- Thank you very much.
- Thanks a lot.

Unit four

(✱ 13) Answer with *yes*.

- Are these your books?
- ▶ *Yes, they are.*
- Yes, they are.

- Is this your newspaper?
- ▶ *Yes, it is.*
- Yes, it is.

- Are those your friends?
- Is this your seat?
- Is that your car?
- Are these your pens?

(✱ 14) Answer with *no*.

- Are these your magazines?
- ▶ *No, they aren't.*
- No, they aren't.

- Is this my newspaper?
- ▶ *No, it isn't.*
- No, it isn't.

- Is that your seat?
- Sorry, is this my glass?
- Excuse me, are these your seats?
- Hey! Are those our seats?

(✱ 15) Make sentences.

- this
- ▶ *Excuse me, this is my seat.*
- Excuse me, this is my seat.

- these
- ▶ *Excuse me, these are our seats.*
- Excuse me, these are our seats.

- that
- those
- these
- this

Unit five

(*16) Answer with *yes*.

- Have they got any money?
- ▶ *Yes, they have.*
- Yes, they have.

- Has she got any sisters?
- ▶ *Yes, she has.*
- Yes, she has.

- Have they got any children?
- Has he got an old car?
- Have you got an 'In English' CD?
- Has she got a boyfriend?

(*17) Answer with *no*.

- Have you got the time?
- ▶ *No, I haven't.*
- No, I haven't.

- Has your car got a CD player?
- ▶ *No, it hasn't.*
- No, it hasn't.

- Have you got a light?
- Has he got an English book?
- Has your book got a DVD with it?
- Have they got cousins?

(*18) Make questions.

- Can I see the doctor?
- ▶ *Have you got an appointment?*
- Have you got an appointment?

- Can my daughter see the dentist?
- ▶ *Has she got an appointment?*
- Has she got an appointment?

- Can my children see the doctor?
- Can my son see the dentist?
- Can I see Mr Smithers?
- Can we see the manager, please?

Unit six

(*19) Make questions.
Repeat.
do   do you   do you do
What do you do?
does   does she   does she do
What does she do?

- he
- ▶ *What does he do?*
- What does he do?

- you
- ▶ *What do you do?*
- What do you do?

- they
- she
- he
- you

(*20) Make negative sentences.

- I – Mondays
- ▶ *I don't work on Mondays.*
- I don't work on Mondays.

- He – Tuesdays
- ▶ *He doesn't work on Tuesdays.*
- He doesn't work on Tuesdays.

- They – Wednesdays
- She – Thursdays
- You – Fridays
- He – Saturdays
- We – Sundays

(*21) Answer with *no*.

- Do you know the answer?
- ▶ *No, I don't know.*
- No, I don't know.

- Does he understand the question?
- ▶ *No, he doesn't understand.*
- No, he doesn't understand.

- Do you know his name?
- Do they know our names?
- Does she understand the grammar?
- Does it work?

Unit seven

(✳22) the /ðə/   the /ðiː/

Repeat.
the   the bank
the   the apple

- Atlantic Ocean
- ▶ *The Atlantic Ocean*
- The Atlantic Ocean

- Pacific Ocean
- ▶ *The Pacific Ocean*
- The Pacific Ocean

- Black Sea
- Irish Sea
- English Channel
- Mississippi River

(✳23) Answer with *yes*.

- Is there a cathedral in the city centre?
- ▶ *Yes, there is.*
- Yes, there is.

- Are there any shops in the village?
- ▶ *Yes, there are.*
- Yes, there are.

- Are there any pubs in the village?
- Is there a shopping mall near the centre?
- Is there a cinema near here?
- Are there any theatres in the city?

(✳24) Make sentences.

Repeat.
there   are   there are   there're

- several museums
- ▶ *There are several museums.*
- There are several museums.

- some tea shops
- two universities
- several theatres
- three shopping malls

Unit eight

(✳25) Timetables

Repeat.
one oh five   two ten   three fifteen
four twenty   five twenty-five   six thirty
seven thirty-five   eight forty   nine forty five
ten fifty   eleven fifty-five   twelve hundred
fifteen thirty   eighteen fifteen
twenty forty-five

(✳26) Clocks

- eleven thirty
- ▶ *Half past eleven.*
- Half past eleven.

- eight forty-five
- ▶ *Quarter to nine.*
- Quarter to nine.

- three fifteen
- twelve oh five
- six fifty-five
- four thirty-five
- two twenty-five
- six thirty
- nine forty-five

(✳27) Departures

- I'm waiting for a flight.
- ▶ *What time does the flight leave?*
- What time does the flight leave?

- I'm waiting for a bus.
- We're waiting for a train.
- She's waiting for a plane.
- He's waiting for a flight.

Unit nine

(✱ 28) Emphasis

- her – me
- ▸ *Don't look at her. Look at me.*
- Don't look at her. Look at me.

- them – us
- her – him
- me – them
- them – her

(✱ 29) Emphasis

- Is it for you or for them?
- ▸ *It isn't for you, it's for them.*
- It isn't for you, it's for them.

- Is it for me or for him?
- ▸ *It isn't for me, it's for him.*
- It isn't for me, it's for him.

- Is it for him or for you?
- Is it for me or for them?
- Is it for us or for her?
- Is it for them or for us?

(✱ 30) Be polite. Add *please*.

- Give it to me.
- ▸ *Please give it to me.*
- Please give it to me.

- Be quiet.
- Don't talk.
- Don't be silly.
- Give them to us.

Unit ten

(✱ 31) Requests

- Please repeat that.
- ▸ *Can you repeat that?*
- Can you repeat that?

- Please translate it.
- Please speak slowly.
- Please get me some water.
- Please spell that word.
- Please write it for me.

(✱ 32) Answer with *no*, then ask.

- Can you run twenty kilometres?
- ▸ *No, I can't. Can you?*
- No, I can't. Can you?

- Can you swim five kilometres?
- Can you speak Welsh?
- Can you type one hundred words a minute?

(✱ 33) Make sentences.

- I can sing.   he
- ▸ *He can sing.*
- He can sing.

- He can sing.   dance
- ▸ *He can dance.*
- He can dance.

- He can dance.   they
- They can dance.   she
- She can dance.   play the piano
- She can play the piano.   you
- You can play the piano.   swim
- You can swim.   we

Unit eleven

✱34 Make questions.

- meat
- ▶ *Is there any meat?*
- Is there any meat?

- potatoes
- ▶ *Are there any potatoes?*
- Are there any potatoes?

- fish
- grapes
- eggs
- milk
- sausages
- cheese

✱35 Answer with *yes*.

Repeat.
there is   there's
there are   there're

- Have we got any milk?
- ▶ *Yes, there's some milk in the fridge.*
- Yes, there's some milk in the fridge.

- Have we got any sausages?
- ▶ *Yes, there are some sausages in the fridge.*
- Yes, there are some sausages in the fridge.

- Have we got any cheese?
- Have we got any eggs?
- Have we got any yoghurt?
- Have we got any strawberries?

✱36 Answer with *no*.

- Can I have some cheese?
- ▶ *No, sorry. There isn't any left.*
- No, sorry. There isn't any left.

- Can I have some more chips?
- ▶ *No, sorry. There aren't any left.*
- No, sorry. There aren't any left.

- Can I have some milk?
- Can I have some grapes?
- Can I have some more bread?

Unit twelve

✱37 Make sentences.

Repeat.
I'd   he'd   she'd   you'd   we'd   they'd
I   I'd   I'd like   I'd like some coffee.

- I – coffee
- ▶ *I'd like some coffee.*
- I'd like some coffee.

- She – tea
- ▶ *She'd like some tea.*
- She'd like some tea.

- They – milk
- I – water
- He – orange juice
- We – tea

✱38 Make questions.

- Which one?
- ▶ *Which one would you like?*
- Which one would you like?

- How much?
- ▶ *How much would you like?*
- How much would you like?

- What?
- How many?
- Which one?
- How much?

✱39 Emphasis

- this one or that one
- ▶ *Would you like this one or that one?*
- Would you like this one or that one?

- regular or large
- ▶ *Would you like regular or large?*
- Would you like regular or large?

- these ones or those ones
- small or large
- tea or coffee
- some of this or some of that

Unit thirteen

(✻40) Answer with *no, thanks*.

- Can I help you?
- ▶ *No, thanks. I'm just looking.*
- No, thanks. I'm just looking.

- May I help you?
- Do you need any help?
- Can I help you?
- Would you like some help?

(✻41) Ask for directions.

- Oxford Street
- ▶ *Excuse me, I'm looking for Oxford Street.*
- Excuse me, I'm looking for Oxford Street.

- The railway station
- The shopping mall
- Bond Street
- an underground station

(✻42) Make statements.

- one
- ▶ *It's on the first floor.*
- It's on the first floor.

- two
- three
- four
- five
- six

(✻43) Make statements.

- three – men's clothes
- ▶ *Men's clothes are on the third floor.*
- Men's clothes are on the third floor.

- five – the restaurant
- ▶ *The restaurant is on the fifth floor.*
- The restaurant is on the fifth floor.

- two – women's clothes
- one – the coffee shop
- four – children's clothes
- five – the restaurant
- three – men's clothes

Unit fourteen

(✻44) Ask questions.

- Sorry. They aren't here now.
- ▶ *What are they doing?*
- What are they doing?

- Sorry. She can't speak to you now.
- ▶ *What's she doing?*
- What's she doing?

- Sorry. I can't talk to you now.
- Sorry. He's busy at the moment.
- Sorry. We can't speak to you now.
- Sorry. She isn't free at the moment.

(✻45) Make negative sentences.

- I
- ▶ *I'm not doing anything.*
- I'm not doing anything.

- You
- ▶ *You aren't doing anything.*
- You aren't doing anything.

- He
- We
- They
- She
- I

(✻46) Answer with *yes*.

- Are you listening?
- ▶ *Yes, I am.*
- Yes, I am.

- Is she working this afternoon?
- ▶ *Yes, she is.*
- Yes, she is.

- Are they watching TV?
- Are you studying English?
- Is he reading his book?
- Are we doing this exercise?

Unit fifteen

(*47) Ask questions.

- dancing
- ▶ *Do you like dancing?*
- Do you like dancing?

- swimming
- eating in restaurants
- meeting people
- travelling by air

(*48) Make positive and negative sentences.

- She – yes   he – no
- ▶ *She likes it, but he doesn't.*
- She likes it, but he doesn't.

- We – yes   they – no
- ▶ *We like it, but they don't.*
- We like it, but they don't.

- You – yes   I – no
- He – yes   she – no
- They – yes   we – no
- I – yes   she – no
- He – yes   they – no

(*49) Answer with *no*.

- Would you like some tea?
- ▶ *No, thanks. I wouldn't. I don't like tea.*
- No, thanks, I wouldn't. I don't like tea.

- Would you like some coffee?
- Would you like some beer?
- Would you like some chips?
- Would you like some cheese?

Unit sixteen

(*50) Months

- January
- ▶ *January is the first month.*
- January is the first month.

- February
- ▶ *February is the second month.*
- February is the second month.

- March
- April
- May
- June
- July
- August
- September
- October
- November
- December

(*51) Ask about tomorrow.

- It's cold today.
- ▶ *Is it going to be cold tomorrow?*
- Is it going to be cold tomorrow?

- It's sunny today.
- It's cloudy today.
- It's windy today.
- It's cold today.

(*52) Ask about tomorrow.

- It's raining now.
- ▶ *Is it going to rain tomorrow?*
- Is it going to rain tomorrow?

- It's snowing now.
- It's thundering now.
- It's raining now.

AUDIO EXERCISES

Unit seventeen

✱53 Dates

- 22/1
- ▶ *The twenty-second of January.*
- The twenty-second of January.

- 30/10
- ▶ *The thirtieth of October.*
- The thirtieth of October.

- 20/4
- 31/5
- 15/7
- 31/8
- 11/6
- 21/2
- 30/3
- 22/11
- 12/9
- 31/12

✱54 Make questions.

Repeat.
was /wəz/ I was here. Was he there? Was she at school?
were /wə/ We were here. Were they there? Were you at school?

- you
- ▶ *Where were you yesterday?*
- Where were you yesterday?

- he
- ▶ *Where was he yesterday?*
- Where was he yesterday?

- they
- it
- she
- you

✱55 Answer with *no*.

- Were you here yesterday?
- ▶ *No, I wasn't.*
- No, I wasn't.

- Were they at school last Sunday?
- ▶ *No, they weren't.*
- No, they weren't.

- Was she here last Saturday?
- Was he with you yesterday?
- Was it cold yesterday?
- Were we busy yesterday?

Unit eighteen

✱56 Respond.

- I went out last night.
- ▶ *Did you? I didn't.*
- Did you? I didn't.

- I saw a great film yesterday.
- We went to a pub last night.
- I met a lot of people yesterday.
- We had a great evening.

✱57 Answer with negatives.

- Did they go on holiday last year?
- ▶ *No, they didn't go on holiday last year.*
- No, they didn't go on holiday last year.

- Did she come to school yesterday?
- ▶ *No, she didn't come to school yesterday.*
- No, she didn't come to school yesterday.

- Did you see a film last night?
- Did he know the answers?
- Did we get any letters this morning?
- Did you buy anything yesterday?

✱58 Repeat.

has – had   go – went   buy – bought
come – came   get – got

✱59 Make positive statements.

- He usually has breakfast at home.
- ▶ *He had breakfast at home yesterday.*
- He had breakfast at home yesterday.

- They usually go home by car.
- ▶ *They went home by car yesterday.*
- They went home by car yesterday.

- She usually has lunch at work.
- They usually go to work by train.
- They usually buy bread at the supermarket.
- He usually comes here by bus.

Unit nineteen

(✱ 60) Ask questions.

- They met in 1998.
- ▶ *Sorry? When did they meet?*
- Sorry? When did they meet?

- They got married in 1999.
- ▶ *Sorry? When did they get married?*
- Sorry? When did they get married?

- She started university in 1997.
- He passed his driving test in 2001.
- They moved to London in 2002.
- She worked in London in 2003.

(✱ 61) Regular past simple

Repeat.
/t/ /t/ /t/ work – worked
like – liked dance – danced
/d/ /d/ /d/ move – moved
listen – listened enjoy – enjoyed
/ɪd/ /ɪd/ /ɪd/ want – wanted
need – needed start – started

(✱ 62) Make positive statements.

- Did you enjoy the meal?
- ▶ *Yes, I enjoyed it.*
- Yes, I enjoyed it.

- Did you like the party?
- ▶ *Yes, I liked it.*
- Yes, I liked it.

- Did you enjoy the film?
- Did you want that drink?
- Did you like the coffee?
- Did you start the new story in the book?
- Did you finish your homework?

(✱ 63) Ask what happened?

- She lost all her money.
- ▶ *Really? What happened?*
- Really? What happened?

- He didn't get any of the answers right.
- She went to hospital last week.
- They got divorced last year.
- The police came to his house last night.

Unit twenty

(✱ 64) Answer with *no*.

- Have you got a cold?
- ▶ *No, I haven't.*
- No, I haven't.

- Did you understand the test?
- ▶ *No, I didn't.*
- No, I didn't.

- Were you there yesterday?
- Do you know them?
- Does she know them?
- Has he got your book?
- Did you see the programme?
- Were they correct?

(✱ 65) Ask questions with *Who?*

- Someone went home.
- ▶ *Who went home?*
- Who went home?

- Someone saw the film.
- ▶ *Who saw the film?*
- Who saw the film?

- Someone phoned the police.
- Someone helped them.
- Someone ran away.
- Someone wrote a message.

(✱ 66) Ask questions with *What?*

- She saw something.
- ▶ *What did she see?*
- What did she see?

- I heard something.

▶ *What did you hear?*
● What did you hear?

● They bought something.
● He got something.
● She wrote something.
● He knew something.

Unit twenty-one

✱ 67 Make sentences.

● I – usually
▶ *I usually get up early.*
● I usually get up early.

● He – never
▶ *He never gets up early.*
● He never gets up early.

● She – always
● They – hardly ever
● He – often
● We – sometimes
● You – never

✱ 68 Ask questions with How often?

● I sometimes have lunch at work.
▶ *How often do you do that?*
● How often do you do that?

● He sometimes comes to school by bicycle.
▶ *How often does he do that?*
● How often does he do that?

● They sometimes go dancing.
● She sometimes plays tennis.
● I sometimes get up late.
● He sometimes works at weekends.

✱ 69 Yes or no?

● Do you ever play tennis?   not often
▶ *No, not often.*
● No, not often.

● Do you ever go to the cinema? sometimes
▶ *Yes, sometimes.*
● Yes, sometimes.

● Do you ever go to bed late? often
● Do you ever play golf? never
● Do you ever do your homework? always
● Do you ever get all the answers right? hardly ever
● Do you ever see your cousins? not often
● Do you ever have breakfast at home? usually

Unit twenty-two

✱ 70 Repeat.

one   once   once a day   once a week   once a month
two   twice   twice a day   twice a week   twice a month
three   three times   three times a day   three times a week   three times a month
four   four times   four times a day   four times a week   four times a month

✱ 71 Make sentences.

● Her skirt's long. Her skirt's grey.
▶ *She's wearing a long grey skirt.*
● She's wearing a long grey skirt.

● His tie's new. His tie's blue.
▶ *He's wearing a new blue tie.*
● He's wearing a new blue tie.

● Her jacket's old. Her jacket's brown.
● Her dress is expensive. Her dress is green.
● His suit's new. His suit's dark blue.

✱ 72 Make sentences.

● Her hair's long. Her hair's blonde.
▶ *She's got long blonde hair.*
● She's got long blonde hair.

● His hair's short. His hair's brown.
▶ *He's got short brown hair.*
● He's got short brown hair.

● His beard's long. His beard's white.
● Her hair's beautiful. Her hair's red.

- His moustache is long. His moustache is black.
- Her hair's short. Her hair's grey.

Unit twenty-three

(*73) Answer with *yes*.

- Have you ever been to a pop concert?
- ▶ *Yes, I have.*
- Yes, I have.

- Has he ever been to New York?
- ▶ *Yes, he has.*
- Yes, he has.

- Has she ever been to London?
- Have you ever been to a circus?
- Have they ever been to Paris?
- Has he ever been to a fortune teller?

(*74) Make questions.

- you – London
- ▶ *Have you ever been to London?*
- Have you ever been to London?

- he – New York
- ▶ *Has he ever been to New York?*
- Has he ever been to New York?

- she – Rome
- they – Paris
- you – England
- he – Canada

(*75) Ask questions.

- I've been to New York.
- ▶ *Have you? When did you go?*
- Have you? When did you go?

- She's been to France.
- ▶ *Has she? When did she go?*
- Has she? When did she go?

- They've been to Canada.
- He's been to Scotland.
- I've been to Australia.
- She's been to Hong Kong.

Unit twenty-four

(*76) Make questions.

- we
- ▶ *What have we done?*
- What have we done?

- she
- ▶ *What has she done?*
- What has she done?

- they
- he
- you
- I
- she

(*77) Ask questions.

- It isn't here.
- ▶ *Where has it gone?*
- Where has it gone?

- They aren't here.
- ▶ *Where have they gone?*
- Where have they gone?

- He isn't here.
- They aren't here.
- It isn't here.
- They aren't here.
- She isn't here.

(*78) Make negative statements.

- Don't open the door.
- ▶ *I haven't opened it.*
- I haven't opened it.

- Don't close your book.
- ▶ *I haven't closed it.*
- I haven't closed it.

- Don't move the chair.
- Don't touch the paint.
- Don't start your dinner.
- Don't open the letter.

Unit twenty-five

(★79) Answer.

- Have you done your homework?
- ▶ *No, I haven't. I'll do it later.*
- No, I haven't. I'll do it later.

- Have you phoned him?
- ▶ *No, I haven't. I'll phone him later.*
- No, I haven't. I'll phone him later.

- Have you finished the work?
- Have you phoned her?
- Have you done the washing-up?
- Have you asked them?

(★80) Make requests.

- Turn it down!
- ▶ *Will you turn it down, please?*
- Will you turn it down, please?

- Help me.
- ▶ *Will you help me, please?*
- Will you help me, please?

- Get me some coffee.
- Answer the phone.
- Turn off the radio.
- Open the window.

(★81) Answer with *no*.

- Will you turn off the radio?
- ▶ *No, I won't.*
- No, I won't.

- Will you give me one hundred euros?
- Will you answer your mobile phone?
- Will you help me with my homework?
- Will you lend me your calculator?

Unit twenty-six

(★82) Repeat.

I   I'll   I'll do it later.
He   He'll   He'll be here soon.
They   They'll   They'll help you.
She   She'll   She'll phone tomorrow.
It   It'll   It'll be late.
We   We'll   We'll see you tomorrow.

(★83) Make sentences.

- I – soon
- ▶ *I'll be there soon.*
- I'll be there soon.

- She – later
- ▶ *She'll be there later.*
- She'll be there later.

- We – tomorrow
- He – next week
- It – soon
- They – in a minute

(★84) Ask questions.

- The journey will take half an hour.
- ▶ *Sorry? How long will it take?*
- Sorry? How long will it take?

- The flight will take four hours.
- The journey will take fifteen minutes.
- The flight will take forty-five minutes.

(★85) Answer with *yes*.

- Will it be OK?
- ▶ *Yes, it will.*
- Yes, it will.

- Will you be on time?
- ▶ *Yes, I will.*
- Yes, I will.

- Will she be early?
- Will it be all right?
- Will they be late?
- Will you arrive on time?

Unit twenty-seven

(✻ 86) Make sentences with superlatives.

- They're all small.
- ▶ *But that one's the smallest.*
- But that one's the smallest.

- They're all good.
- ▶ *But that one's the best.*
- But that one's the best.

- They're all big.
- They're all good.
- They're all old.
- They're all bad.

(✻ 87) Make sentences with superlatives.

- They're all important.
- ▶ *But that one's the most important.*
- But that one's the most important.

- They're all successful.
- ▶ *But that one's the most successful.*
- But that one's the most successful.

- They're all popular.
- They're all expensive.
- They're all famous.
- They're all important.

(✻ 88) Make sentences with comparatives.

- he / old / me
- ▶ *He's older than me.*
- He's older than me.

- They / young / us
- ▶ *They're younger than us.*
- They're younger than us.

- She / tall / him
- He / short / her
- I / old / you
- We / young / them

Unit twenty-eight

(✻ 89) Answer with *yes*.

- Have you met him before?
- ▶ *Yes, I have.*
- Yes, I have.

- Does she like him?
- ▶ *Yes, she does.*
- Yes, she does.

- Will he be here soon?
- Can she drive?
- Did he like the birthday present?
- Were they friends?
- Has she seen the film yet?

(✻ 90) Answer with positive sentences.

- Did she speak quietly?
- ▶ *Yes, she spoke quietly.*
- Yes, she spoke quietly.

- Did he close the door quickly?
- ▶ *Yes, he closed the door quickly.*
- Yes, he closed the door quickly.

- Did he speak loudly?
- Did he leave immediately?
- Did he work quietly?
- Did he go immediately?

(✻ 91) Make sentences.

- She was lonely.   always
- ▶ *She was always lonely.*
- She was always lonely.

- They're tired.   usually
- ▶ *They're usually tired.*
- They're usually tired.

- He's angry.   often
- She was unhappy.   sometimes
- They were late.   never
- He's ill.   hardly ever
- We're busy.   usually

Unit twenty-nine

(✳ 92) Make questions.

Repeat.
have to   have to

- He had to work late.
- ▶ *Did you have to work late?*
- Did you have to work late?

- He had to get up early.
- ▶ *Did you have to get up early?*
- Did you have to get up early?

- He had to wear a uniform.
- He had to learn English.
- He had to work at weekends.
- He had to do homework.

(✳ 93) Answer with *had to*.

- Why couldn't they come to the party?
- ▶ *Because they had to work.*
- Because they had to work.

- Why couldn't she go to the concert?
- ▶ *Because she had to work.*
- Because she had to work.

- Why couldn't he go out last Saturday?
- Why couldn't they come to lunch?
- Why couldn't she see us last weekend?
- Why couldn't you go out yesterday?

(✳ 94) Answer with *no*.

- Could she get a ticket?
- ▶ *No, she couldn't.*
- No, she couldn't.

- Could you answer the questions?
- ▶ *No, I couldn't.*
- No, I couldn't.

- Could you get a reply?
- Could he come to the party?
- Could she find her book?
- Could they understand the instructions?

Unit thirty

(✳ 95) Make sentences.

- He wanted to get some money.
- ▶ *So he went to get some money.*
- So he went to get some money.

- She wanted to buy a CD.
- ▶ *So she went to buy a CD.*
- So she went to buy a CD.

- They wanted to do some shopping.
- He wanted to see the doctor.
- She wanted to have a haircut.
- They wanted to change some money.

(✳ 96) Make sentences.

- They
- ▶ *They've gone to get some money.*
- They've gone to get some money.

- He
- ▶ *He's gone to get some money.*
- He's gone to get some money.

- They
- She
- He
- They

(✳ 97) Apologize for leaving.

- Would you like another drink?
- ▶ *Sorry. I've got to go.*
- Sorry. I've got to go.

- Let's have another coffee.
- Do you want some more tea?
- Sit down, I'll put on a video.
- Would you like something to eat?
- Let's do another audio exercise.

ACKNOWLEDGEMENTS

The Publisher and Authors would like to thank the many teachers and institutions who piloted this material in Brazil, China, Eire, France, Hungary, Italy, Japan, Mexico, Poland, Spain, and the UK.

Authors' Acknowledgements:
In a complex series like this, which has taken several years to prepare, pilot and produce, many people are involved and have creative input. We wish to thank the many people at OUP who participated in making this book.

We would like to add our further personal thanks to, Catherine Smith and Karen Jamieson (Project Managers and Student's Book editors), Sally Cooke (Editor, 3 in 1 Practice pack, Teacher's Book and Photocopiables), and Richard Morris (Designer for all components).

Illustrations by:
Kate Charlesworth: p.8
Mark Duffin: pp.34, 35
Uldis Klavins: p.37
Roger Penwill: pp.24, 28, 39, 56

Commissioned photographs by:
Peter Viney: pp.11, 15, 22, 26, 57, 63, 64, 69

The publishers would like to thank the following for their kind permission to reproduce photographs:
Corbis UK Ltd. pp.43 (c) (Bettmann), 43 (r) (Bettmann), 48 (Bettmann), 49 (t) (Peter Turnley); Oxford University Press pp.13, 17 (c), 17 (t), 21 (l), 29 (bl), 29 (cl), 31, 33, 38, 67; Oxford University Press/Hemera pp.12, 16, 18 (all), 19, 20, 21 (c), 21 (r), 29 (br), 29 (cr), 29 (tl), 29 (tr), 30 (all), 32, 36, 41 (all), 50, 51, 52 (b), 52 (t), 54, 55 (all), 59 (all), 60, 62, 68; NASA p.49 (b); Richard Morris p.14; PA Photos p.46 (EPA PHOTO/DPA Volker DORNBERGER); Rex Features pp.17 (b) (Dezo Hoffmann), 42 (l) (Everett Collection), 42 (r), 43 (l) (News International); Science Photo Library p.42 (c) (Novosti); Zooid Pictures pp.45 (l), 45 (r)